This Book

presented to the

CHURCH LIBRARY IN MEMORY OF

Mother of Casey Deshon

BY

Birdville Baptist Church

Code 4386-23, No. 3, Broadman Supplies, Nashville, Tenn. Printed in USA

A Gardener Looks at the Fruits of the Spirit

By the same author . . .

A Shepherd Looks at Psalm 23
A Layman Looks at the Lord's Prayer
A Shepherd Looks at the Good Shepherd and His Sheep
Mountain Splendor
Rabboni
As a Tree Grows
Expendable
Gideon—Mighty Man of Valor
Charles Bowen—Paul Bunyan of the West
Splendour from the Sea
Taming Tension

W. Phillip Keller

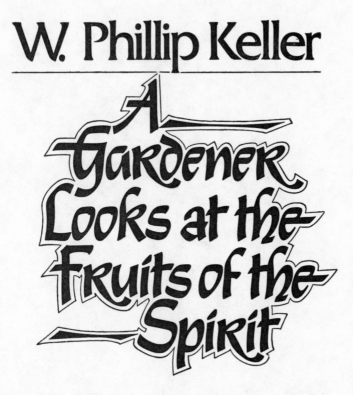

A Gardener Looks at the Fruits of the Spirit

WORD BOOKS
PUBLISHER
WACO, TEXAS

To
URSULA
MY COURAGEOUS COMPANION
ALONG LIFE'S TOUGH TRAILS

Contents

Introduction

It was at the special invitation of Mr. Al Bryant, senior editor of Word Books, that this book was written. He has waited patiently during its preparation. I am grateful to God that the material shared in the pages that follow, when first shared with my congregation, was used by God's Gracious Spirit to lead some into a more intimate life with Christ. May the same be true for you the reader.

Various books, pamphlets, and articles have been published dealing with the fruits of God's Spirit. These have been very beneficial to Christians and have contributed richly to the lives of those who earnestly longed to be conformed to the character of Christ. It is my genuine hope and prayer that this will be true of this book.

The approach taken in this work, rather than being predominantly doctrinal, is very practical and deals more directly with the *how* and *why* of fruit production in our lives. As with some of my other books such as *A Shepherd Looks at Psalm 23, A Layman Looks at the Lord's Prayer, Rabboni, A Shepherd Looks at the Good Shepherd and His Sheep, As a Tree Grows,* and so on, it is written in plain layman's language.

The approach taken here is based upon the overall teaching of both the Old and New Testaments. There God's people are likened to a carefully cultivated garden. This piece of ground is tended and tilled with tender, loving care. It is watered, hedged, and husbanded with undivided devotion. God Himself in Christ by His Spirit is the Gardener. He comes looking for fruit.

Sometimes He gathers a bountiful harvest.

Sometimes the returns and response to all His efforts are minimal.

The reasons for this are dealt with in great detail in the first four chapters included under *Part I: Four Types of Soil.* This section is based on our Lord's own teaching in the parable of the sower found in the Gospels.

The individual fruits of the Spirit, and how they are produced, are then treated in *Part II: The Nine Facets of God's Love.* This section is drawn from the writings of Paul based particularly on the well-known passages in 1 Corinthians 13 and Galatians 5, where the fruits are listed.

In each case the individual attribute of God's own

love, of His very life, is examined from three aspects:

1) Its function in God's own character, and how this determines His attitudes and actions toward us.

2) The growth of this fruit in our own lives and its effect upon both God Himself and others around us.

3) How it can be encouraged and cultivated in abundant measure.

From the foregoing it will be seen that a study is made of both the quantity and quality of fruit production in a Christian's life. An earnest endeavor is here made to instruct the reader in the great basic principles of fruit production.

As Henry Drummond stated clearly so long ago, fruits and flowers do not just grow by caprice in the natural realm, nor do the fruits of God's Spirit flourish in our own lives by mere whimsy or accident. Certain causes produce certain effects both in the natural and spiritual realms. It is as we begin to see that concept in Christian living that a whole new exciting life like Christ's can open up to us.

Because unnumbered millions of men and women (whether in the country or in the city) are gardeners, they will readily identify with the ideas presented here. Anyone who, like myself, loves the soil, enjoys gardening, revels in plants and shrubs, crops and trees will follow these pages with ease—and I trust pleasure.

Most of all may this book enrich your life in God beyond measure!

PART ONE

Four Types of Soil

ONE

Pathway People — for the Birds

1

In that delightful romance, "The Song of Solomon" in the Old Testament, we are given a glimpse of God's view of His garden. He calls His chosen people, His bride, the Church, you and I, His garden.

There in pure, powerful, poetic language He draws for us a word picture of the enormous pleasure and delight He derives from His garden of herbs and spices, fruits and flowers. He longs for it to be a rich source of satisfaction to Him who loves and tends us with His everlasting diligence and care:

> A garden inclosed is my sister,
> my spouse; a spring shut up,
> a fountain sealed.
>
> Thy plants are an orchard of
> pomegranates, with pleasant fruits;
> camphire, with spikenard,

15

Spikenard and saffron; calamus
and cinnamon, with all trees
of frankincense; myrrh and aloes,
with all the chief spices:

A fountain of gardens, a well of
living waters, and streams from Lebanon.

Awake, O north wind; and come,
thou south; blow upon my garden,
that the spices thereof may flow out.
Let my beloved come into his garden,
and eat his pleasant fruits.
Song of Solomon 4:12–16

Like so many things in life, this is the ideal, the ultimate which God has in His heart for us. It is the deepest desire of His Spirit for us—that toward which so much of the energy and activity of His life is directed. He comes to us seeking for the fruits, the fragrant attributes of His own careful cultivation in our characters.

Sometimes He is distinctly disappointed.

There is no fruitage.

Or if there is, it is sparse and sickly.

Despite His most diligent endeavors there is a dearth of production.

In fact, again and again He bemoans the feeble growth and the fickle flowering which results in only meager, shrunken, shriveled fruit.

At times there spring up wild varieties in the garden of our lives: wild vines and untamed weeds.

On other occasions there is simply no crop at all. Why? Because basically there are such things as non-productive soils and marginal land.

Of these, the first which our Lord described were the wayside soils: the land along the paths that had been beaten hard by the passing feet of those who crisscrossed it in their travels.

Anyone familiar with Africa, the Middle East, or the Orient, will quickly grasp the picture. Here multitudes of poor people struggle to wrest a meager living from tiny plots of land. Scattered across the countryside in an irregular patchwork the little gardens are transected and crisscrossed with a weblike network of tiny footpaths.

It is along these thin trails that men and women bear their burdens traveling to and fro across the countryside. Along these primitive paths, beaten hard as pavement by uncounted passing feet, children race and run and play their games. Along these paths, back and forth, move the donkeys, mules, camels, and caravans of commerce.

It was along these pathways as a boy that I ran barefooted and carefree, like the wind, growing up in Africa's sunshine.

It was along these trails that I later strode, traversing the country in search of game to feed my family. These paths were the trails leading into new terrain and high adventure over beckoning hills on the horizon.

But the soil trodden by my feet and those of ten thousand other passers-by, had become hard as brick, solid as cement, and impervious to the thrusting young roots of any seed sown upon it.

Jesus Himself had tramped hundreds of miles under the heat of the summer sun along such paths.

His feet had become dusty with the soil scuffed up under His sandals. Often He had seen the stray seed lying loose along the path. There it remained ungerminated, unmoving, unproductive.

It was a waste of seed, a waste of the gardener's energy to scatter it on such soil. It was a waste of hope to think there would ever be any crop. Such ground was good only for the birds. There they quickly spotted the seed lying bare and exposed. It was easy to fly down and snatch it away. The end result was bareness.

Jesus said some of our lives were like that soil.

He called us "Pathway People." The garden of our lives had, in places, been beaten hard as rock by the passing to and fro of other people and influences in our experience.

He did not elaborate upon who those strangers and visitors may have been. Obviously He could not begin to enumerate or catalogue them all. For with each garden plot they would differ. But for all of us there are certain people and influences that beat a path through our lives. Here are some of them. All can harden our hearts in such a way that there is little or no response to the Word of God which may have been planted there. The first includes:

1) Our friends and associates.

It may well be asked, "Who are the people who most frequently pound a path through my life?"

"What sort of impact do they make upon my mind?"

"Are they hardening me against God?"

18

"Do they compact and compress my convictions against Christ?"

"Are they slowly solidifying my sentiments against the Gracious Spirit of God?"

These are perfectly proper and appropriate questions which we need to face. Often, quite unknown to ourselves, our souls are being set against the very One who tends us with such loving attention.

Christ comes to us in compassion to implant the seed of His own special Word. He endeavors to cultivate the soil of our lives by the inner working of His own gentle Spirit. But He runs into resistance. The soil has been hardened by the impaction of a thousand other passers-by.

The trail that has been trodden across my spirit and soul is solidified by the world's ideologies and thoughts. I become conditioned by the culture of my society.

When God's view of things is laid upon my heart, when His claims are brought to bear upon me, my initial response often is, "Forget it—that's strictly for the birds."

This is why, whenever it is my joy to lead someone to Christ, one of my greatest concerns is that they should quickly establish a new circle of Christian friends and associates. They can no longer afford to allow just any strangers or alien associates to beat a path through their lives.

If they do, the results can be disastrous both for them and for God. Those who do not know Christ can so condition their outlook and set their minds

19

against the Savior that there is stern resistance to God's Word when presented to them. There is no warm response of obedience to the overtures of the Gracious Spirit. So the ground of their lives lies bare and unproductive. The good seed of God's Word cannot germinate in such a situation. Whatever is said is snatched away by the enemy of men's souls. There is no fruit.

The attitude is one of total indifference. "That's just a bunch of nonsense—forget it—it's for the birds."

2) The literature that we read and the T.V. programs we watch.

The second strong influence which beats a path through our lives is the reading or viewing material to which we allow our minds and emotions to be exposed. What sort of books do I read? What kind of magazines, journals, and newspapers do I digest? What type of television or radio programs do I follow?

In this whole area we are more often than not creatures of habit. We acquire certain insatiable appetites and preferences for special periodicals, programs or professional performers. In fact, they become almost a mania. We allow ourselves to be manipulated by the mass media, becoming like clay in the hands of the author, writer or producer. We are pounded and compacted by the relentless pressures that play upon us until our convictions set like cement.

Many of the men and women who dominate the

media either in publishing or programing are non-Christians. Some are violently anti-God. Such set out in subtle but severe ways to undermine and destroy the quiet faith of God's people. Through means of insidious suggestions, doubt, disparagement, and despair they endeavor to undermine our confidence in Christ.

The total tragedy of all this is that steadily and surely certain patterns of worldly thought and philosophy beat their way through our lives. As Solomon, the great Sage, wrote long centuries ago: "There is a way which seemeth right unto a man, but the end thereof are the ways of death!" (Prov. 14:12).

In the garden of our inner lives that death is utter fruitlessness. God's ideas, God's economy, God's view of life, God's standards of behavior, God's priorities simply cannot penetrate our hard hearts. There is no way the good seed of His Word can ever germinate or take root in such stubborn soil set against Him.

In the end, we are the sum total of all our own choices. The decisions as to what I shall allow my mind, emotions, will, and spirit to be exposed to rests with me. Whether or not my life shall be intractable or mellow under God's good hand in large part depends upon who I permit to beat a path through it.

3) The music we listen to constantly.

This constitutes a third problem area. It may come as somewhat of a shock to some readers to discover that the wrong sort of music can harden us against God.

Many kinds of music are highly commendable. Some of the very first music played out upon the planet was composed under the exquisite inspiration of God's own Spirit.

The majestic sounds of surf on sand or thundering waterfalls and tumbling streams. The mellow melodies of wind in the trees or breezes blowing across the grasslands. The gentle notes of bird song, insects in the meadow, a child's laughter or an old man's plaintive whistle all can lift our spirits.

Yet at the same time there is hard, harsh music. Coming out of the contorted culture of men apart from God, it depicts and reflects the fierce emotions and passionate despair of men in darkness. It creates enormous stress and impassioned emotions with its relentless beat.

If allowed to do so, it also can beat its way into the very personality of people. In the hands of evil men it is capable of enormous damage to the minds and emotions of the young. Noble convictions and lofty restraints can be broken down through the implacable pounding of "mad" music.

One of its most insidious dangers is that it distracts men and women from the things of God's Spirit. Instead they become fascinated with the old natural life. Their emotions are aroused and their passions inflamed. The whole personality may be set upon a perverse way of conduct contrary to God's best intentions for His children.

Unfortunately some of this music now passes

amongst God's people as acceptable. Little do some realize how seriously they have been deluded. Their affections have been taken captive and their wills have been set hard against God.

4) The pursuit of pleasure.

It is true to say that in large measure we of the west are a hedonistic society . . . a people totally given over to the pursuit of pleasure, ease, and luxury. For many, pleasure itself has become the main preoccupation in life. To indulge one's self in some sort of sensual experience has become a mania.

As with music, so with pleasure, some pursuits are noble, commendable, and inspiring. Others can be decidedly debasing and destructive. The parent fondling and loving a child experiences pleasure and benefits both himself (herself) and the family. But the parent who gambles away his (her) earnings does a serious disservice to the whole home.

Pleasures of so many sorts can become an obsession. They tyrannize our time and dominate our days. Their constant demands upon us begin to beat a path through the brief span of our little lives. Such pleasures command so much of our thought, energy, and means that those areas they control are land in our lives lost to God.

If the resources devoted to pleasure were given over instead to Christ's interests in the world, we would indeed be amazed. Congregations would flourish. Churches would be crowded. Missionaries would multiply. The poor would be helped. The downtrodden would be lifted up. The suffering of earth's men and women would be alleviated. And like our Master Himself, many would go about doing this weary old world a great deal of good.

Our Father, the Gardener of our lives, looks for friable soil in which to produce such graces. But sad to say, sometimes our days are so packed with pleasure they pass without producing a single fruit of benevolence that will endure throughout eternity. We are too preoccupied.

5) Our personal ambitions.

The whole subject of personal, private ambitions poses an enormous problem for many Christians. They struggle relentlessly to accommodate their own desires to the great will of God. There is within them a tension between attaining their own ends and serving Christ.

Ambition of the right sort—putting God first in all of our affairs—seeking above all else to please Him while serving others—is a powerful implement in the hand of God for producing rich fruit in our lives and the lives of others. It breaks up the hardness of a heart set on only selfish ends. It redirects the enthusiasm and energy of the whole person into fields of usefulness.

But by the same measure the individual with strong personal ambitions of self-centeredness is soon set against God. It is an inexorable principle that any ambition established deep within our wills becomes the polestar of our daily decisions. All our choices, whether conscious or unconscious, are trimmed toward that one end. It becomes the over-riding consideration that pounds out a predominant path through all our activities.

All else becomes secondary, even Christ's claims upon us.

It is for this reason that the word of the Lord through Jeremiah was: "Seekest thou great things for thyself? Seek them not" (Jer. 45:5).

In bold contrast our Lord's admonition was: "Seek ye first the kingdom of God, and his righteousness; and all these things shall be added unto you" (Matt. 6:33).

6) Our private thought life.

It has been well said that "I am what I think about when alone—not what I pretend to be in public." That is a most sobering and searching statement. It strips away the façade and false front.

This is the way God, our Father, knows and sees us.

He alone has carefully examined, explored, and investigated every square foot of the little garden of our lives. Having gone over all the ground with great care, He alone knows that there are some areas, some beaten pathways where He simply cannot get a single seed of His own gracious life to grow.

Perhaps more often than anything else, the ground of our persistent old thought patterns is the toughest soil He has ever had to tackle. Some of us harbor places where unforgiven grudges and grievances have hardened against others across the years. Even the dynamite of His Holy Spirit can scarcely break up the compacted clods of scorn, censure, and cruel hostility that harden us.

In some lives belligerence, animosity, and illwill have beaten a trail through our thinking for so long that not a single good seed dropped there by the Gracious Spirit of God can ever grow. The same wretched old thoughts have set our souls brick hard.

If anyone suggests to us that we should change our inner attitudes or animosity we grunt in disgust and shrug off the idea with the crass comment, "That's strictly for the birds."

God's Word states pragmatically: "As he thinketh in his heart, so is he!" (Prov. 23:7). For those who think hard thoughts, there lies hard soil that will not yield to God's good care.

Only the deepest convicting work of God's Gracious Spirit in the soul can begin to alter such tough soil. And until that happens no fruit of godliness can come from that ground.

7) The Master's footprints.

There is a very ancient saying in agriculture that "The finest fertilizer on a gardener's ground are his own footprints."

The attentive, enthusiastic gardener does not, like strangers and outsiders, limit himself just to the pathways. His feet do not pound and abuse the same places with their persistent passing. Rather he moves gently, tenderly, and carefully over every square foot of ground. He knows each tree, plant, shrub, and flower that flourishes on his land. He literally loves them into abundant profusion and rich production.

If anyone is to walk through my life, it should be He who tends me, cares for me, knows all about me, and longs to improve the garden of my life. This is none other than God Himself. He is the great and good gardener, the Husbandman who loves me.

This is a picture of Jesus Christ. By His gracious, kindly Spirit, He moves in our lives sharing His very own life with us. Pouring out His benefits and blessings upon us, He works deep within our spirits to mellow us and make us receptive to His own good seed. He enables us to respond to the implanting of His own new life from above. As He introduces the exotic fruits of His own person into the prepared soil of our hearts, there they take root and flourish.

The final choice as to who or what shall dominate the garden of my life pretty much depends on me. God does not choose my friends, my reading material, my music, my pleasures, my ambitions or my thoughts for me. I do this.

The ultimate question simply is: "Do I or don't I want to be a 'pathway person'? Will I allow the Master's footprints to enrich the soil of my soul? Or do I prefer to let worldly ways harden my soul against His good plan for my life?"

TWO

Rocky People without Deep Roots

The second type of soil which our Lord discussed was rocky or stony ground. In modern terminology we would refer to this as marginal soil. This is soil which, even though cleared and cultivated at enormous cost and with infinite care, often produces only pathetic results. This is true because it is so stony.

One can find fields of this sort all over the earth. In my travels to some forty countries around the world I have always been deeply moved by the enormous labors of peasant people to clear rocky land for crops. I have seen this throughout the Middle East, in parts of Africa, along the Mediterranean littoral, in the British Isles, in the Eastern Provinces of Canada, in Mexico and even the Hawaiian Islands, to name a few. Small parcels of stony soil are surrounded with sturdy walls of rock lifted and cleared from the difficult ground with enormous toil, sweat, and diligence by the loving owners.

Christ was familiar with scenes such as these. Often in His travels across the Palestinian countryside He had tramped the dusty tracks that traversed the rocky hillsides where farmers fought to wrest a few meager handfuls of grain from the stony ground. He had sometimes seen a small patch of rock-riddled land glow green with the empty promise of a flourishing crop. Yet a few days or weeks later under the blazing summer sun the crop had shriveled, scorched and seared. Without deep roots the planting perished, leaving the work-worn owner with nothing but broken hopes and a mere remnant of shrunken produce.

No doubt, too, while working in His dusty little carpenter shop in Nazareth, He, the Master Craftsman, had been asked to repair and rebuild many a plow broken and battered on the boulders of some tough hillside land.

Surrounded by such reminders of rocky ground He had often reflected on the winsome Old Testament passages where, through the prophets, God had likened His people to stony ground.

A new heart also will I give you, and a new spirit will I put within you: and I will take away the stony heart out of your flesh, and I will give you an heart of flesh. And I will put my spirit within you, and cause you to walk in my statutes, and ye shall keep my judgments, and do them. And ye shall dwell in the land that I gave to your fathers; and ye shall be my people, and I will be your God. I will also save you from all your uncleannesses: and I will call for the corn, and will increase it, and lay no famine upon you. And I will multiply the fruit of the tree, and the increase of the field, that ye shall receive no more reproach of famine among the heathen. Then shall ye remember your own evil ways, and your doings that were not good, and shall loathe yourselves in your own sight for your iniquities and for your abominations. Not for your sakes do I this, saith the Lord God, be it known unto you: be ashamed and confounded for your own ways, O house of Israel.

Thus saith the Lord God; In the day that I shall have cleansed you from all your iniquities I will also cause you to dwell in the cities, and the wastes shall be builded. And the desolate land shall be tilled, whereas it lay desolate in the sight of all that passed by. And they shall say, This land that was desolate is become like the garden of Eden; and the waste and desolate and ruined cities are become fenced, and are inhabited. Then the heathen that are left round about you shall know that I the Lord build the ruined places, and plant that that was desolate: I the Lord have spoken it, and I will do it.

(Ezek. 36:26–36)

There in majestic language and heart-stirring strains the great prophet of His people had predicted what He Himself would accomplish for those whom He referred to as His garden. The land which lay desolate would be redeemed, restored, brought back into productivity. The stony soil of their souls would be salvaged and made soft and friable. An incredible transformation would take place in the tough terrain of their hard hearts. And this bit of barren ground

31

would eventually flourish like a glorious garden of Eden.

As our Lord pondered these great prophecies He knew they would come true. It could not be otherwise under the deep and diligent care of the divine gardener. It was He who saw the potential productivity lying dormant in desolate human hearts. Only He could transform the toughest soul into a gorgeous garden. As the Great Gardener He was prepared to tackle this task for His own name's sake. His reputation was at stake in the project.

These were the thoughts uppermost in our Lord's mind when He declared flatly that some of us were hard, rocky people. The reason virtually no fruit was produced in our experience was simply that we are such stony souls.

Now you may very well ask in sincerity, "What constitutes a 'stony soul'? What are the characteristics of a rocky character? What sort of conduct or behavior belies the boulders buried beneath the surface of an unproductive life? What are the earmarks of 'marginal land' that spell out crop failures?"

Before dealing with these difficulties in our lives we must pause briefly and reflect on God's view of the absolute necessity for fruit production in the lives of His people. On a number of occasions our Lord made it abundantly clear to His hearers that the final criteria by which His own were known was fruitfulness. "You shall know them by their fruit."

He told various parables portraying the care, love, and expertise applied by the Divine Gardener to His

orchards, vineyards, fields, and crops. He emphasized dramatically that the husbandman, the cultiva-
tor, came looking for a crop. And unless there was
fruitage the whole enterprise was a total disaster.
Crop failures simply could not be tolerated.

In the Christian experience, and in the church as
a whole, this fact has often been forgotten. There
is a distinct tendency to sidestep this whole issue
by involving ourselves in other activities which we
seem to believe will cover up our barrenness.

We are not known, either to God or to a skeptical
society around us, as Christians based on what we
claim to believe. Nor are we identified with Christ
just by the creed to which we may subscribe. We
are not recognized as God's garden by some special
ecstatic or supernatural experience we may have en-
joyed. Our profound biblical insight or great grasp
of Scripture does not make us of consequence in
His economy.

We are identified and known by the sort of fruit,
the quantity of fruit, and the quality of fruit borne
out in our daily conversation, conduct, and character.
There is no greater criterion for Christians. It is the
paramount gauge of God's people.

This being the case, what then constitutes rocky
ground—unproductive soil? As in nature, so in
our lives, there are three major types of marginal
land.

The first of these includes those deceptive areas
where only a thin layer of soil lies over a vast expanse
of basement rock (so-called bedrock). Millennia of
weathering of the original substrata of stone has

served to sheath the basement formations of rock with a shallow skin of sickly soil.

Seed dropped into such shallow soil will spring up quickly. Rocks retain both heat and moisture. So in this apparently favorable ground the seedlings appear to get off to a quick start.

Sad to say, the sudden burst of green growth is short lived. The fragile roots of the young plants run into rocky resistance. They cannot grow. There is no place to go—no depth of nourishing soil from which they can derive nourishment. There is no space in which to spread and expand their root system.

Under the heat of spring sunshine and the searing rays of intense sunlight the tender plants soon succumb. They wilt, begin to turn gray, then yellow, then brown until finally bleached and beaten by the heat, they collapse—a crop failure.

Jesus said some of us are like that.

The good seed of His Word is dropped into the shallow soil of our superficial souls. It seems to be an attractive area. At first there is a positive response. We seem to flourish. Our new Christian friends; our warm loving fellowship; our somewhat ecstatic experiences; our fresh encounters produce a sudden flush of new growth that just as quickly starts to shrivel up and wither away.

Suddenly we realize that it has been a superficial show, a "surface experience." The whole process has been painfully pathetic. The person who started off with such promise has petered out. The one who appeared to have such enormous potential for fruit production has fallen by the way. We are dismayed, and God, the Good Gardener, is disappointed.

What is the profound problem here?

What is the difficulty lying below the surface of our apparently spiritual lives?

It can be stated in a single word—*Unbelief.*

Unbelief is one of the most difficult subjects to deal with in a book of this kind. Like the massive formations of bedrock that underlie some marginal land, because it is out of sight, hidden from view, it almost defies exposure. Yet it underlies so many of our lives.

An honest attempt will be made here to deal with what unbelief is and how it stunts and shrivels us.

There are three formidable dimensions to unbelief which, if we can grasp them, will enable us to see what our spiritual soil is really like.

The first of these is this: when we come into contact with Christianity initially our belief is not really in Christ, but rather in the church. By the church I mean the pastor, the preacher, the evangelist, the counselor, the congregation, the liturgy, the fellowship, the friendship, the experiences, the sharing, the love of other so-called Christians, the acceptance and concern of God's family.

All of these are to be commended. Each plays its part in leading us to Christ. All nurture us as newborn people. But these factors are not and can never be used as a substitute for God Himself. Our faith, our belief, our trust, if invested only in the church, its people and its programs will lead to disillusionment, discouragement, and despair.

Our belief, our trust, our confidence, our faith must find its foundation in God. He is the only ground of our salvation, of our deliverance, of our hope, of our peace, of our very life.

So many of us have the roots of our faith in the shallow soil of the social life of the Christian community of which we are part. Because of this we are sure to be shaken. Preachers and teachers may prove to be less than perfect. The support and friendship of other Christians may play us false. The liturgy or social functions of the church may go flat. And since we ourselves are a part of all this the spiritual soil of our lives is soon seen to be shallow.

When things go wrong we grow hard and cynical. We find ourselves being set like stone against that which is godly. Basically all of this happens because our hope, our trust, our confidence was not in Christ, but in the church. And often when the heat is on, the church simply does not sustain us in the stress of our society and times.

On the other hand, Christ has never betrayed any confidence placed in Him. He always validates any faith or trust vested in Him. Yet most of us simply do not believe this or Him. This is what makes it so difficult for Him to produce His fruit in our lives.

Christ comes to us continually by His Gracious Spirit, inviting us quietly to put our implicit and undivided confidence in Himself. But this we decline to do. We are reluctant to trust Him—even with the most common details of our lives. We will trust and we will try almost anything or anyone else . . . but not Him.

This bedrock of unbelief in the living person of the living God is what makes it virtually impossible for Him to produce any sort of eternal, enduring results (fruit) in our lives.

The second dimension of unbelief is our refusal to actually believe God's Word. Because we do not really consider the Bible to be a valid, documentary declaration of divine truth, we question the credibility of the Scriptures. We refuse to recognize them as a supernatural revelation of spiritual integrity.

Too many of us equate the Scriptures with other writings of human origin. Naively we assume that it is our personal preogative to accept or reject them. We consider it really not mandatory that we respond to their declarations by prompt and positive action.

The net result is that at every point where they have spoken to us and we have neglected to react as we should, the unbelief of our hearts (our wills) hardens us. It is no small wonder that Scripture repeatedly speaks of the hardness of men's hearts . . . the unwillingness of their wills to cooperate and comply with the will and wishes of God.

The enormous subsurface resistance of our subconscious minds and wills to the best intentions of God is terrifying. It is little wonder that in some lives, despite His most tender care and concern, there is nothing but a crop failure.

Let me illustrate. The Word of God instructs us emphatically to live at peace with others, in so far as it is possible. This admonition is repeated over and over. If in defiance of such directives we deliberately determine to have an ongoing vendetta with someone else, there will be *no peace.*

This fruit of God's Gracious Spirit will not be present. It will be a total failure. Not because God is an incompetent gardener, but because of the rocky resistance of my own hard will.

The third dimension to *unbelief* is our formidable preoccupation with *self.* From earliest childhood we are taught and trained to be self-reliant, self-confident, self-promoting people. *I* and *me* and *my* are the triune epicenter around which our little lives revolve. We build our entire earthly sojourn upon the premise that *myself* is the most important person upon the planet. The net result is *self-centeredness* of appalling proportions.

Moving in a diametrically opposite direction comes the call of Christ to us to forget ourselves (lose our lives); to follow Him (that is, put Him at the heart and center of our affairs); and give ourselves in glad service to others.

It all goes very much against our grain. We may not say so publicly, but privately we are convinced this is the sure path to oblivion and nothingness. *We really do not believe that God in Christ has the only formula for a fulfilling and abundant life.*

The simple consequence is that though mentally and perhaps even emotionally we may claim to believe Christ, deep down in our wills, dispositions, and spirits we do not. We regard Him as an idealist not truly worthy of our undivided allegiance, loyalty, and confidence. In such stony souls underlain by incredible unbelief the Spirit of God strives in vain to produce the fruits of His own winsome character.

There are three simple steps that can be taken to break up our unbelief under the dynamic impulse of God's Spirit.

1) Ask God in sincerity to show you Himself. Ask Him to let you see what He is really like. When you discover that He is the Good Gardener who loves you immensely and longs to make your life productive it will pulverize your proud stony heart.

2) Ask Christ by His Spirit to show you yourself and the hard condition of your own inner will. When it dawns upon your dull soul how defiant and difficult you can be, it will break your heart and prepare it for His deep work.

3) Ask God by His Spirit to impart to you great faith— the faith to trust Him implicitly; the faith to have complete confidence in Christ and in His commitments to us; the faith of obedience to simply step out and do whatever He asks by His Spirit through His Word.

The second type of rocky ground is what we generally call stony soil. This is land littered with loose stones and boulders varying in size from that of large eggs to random rocks weighing hundreds of pounds. Frequently this is very fertile soil which requires enormous labor and expense to clear for proper cultivation.

My boyhood home in the heart of Africa was located on such land. My father had acquired 110 acres of desolate land on a high ridge. With tremendous toil, using teams of oxen, he literally tore thousands of stones from the ground. In fact they were numerous enough to build all the walls of all the buildings he erected on the property. And where the stones had lain there were planted thousands of trees of all sorts—fruit trees, coffee trees, ornamental trees, and firewood trees. Gorgeous gardens, too, and luxuriant pastures for cattle, replaced what previously had been desolate and derelict land. It was in fact a down-to-earth demonstration of the prophecy foretold by Ezekiel. It was a garden of Eden flourishing where before there had been nothing but stones, scrub thorn, and the cry of the jackals in the wilderness.

In the Christian experience there are likewise wilderness areas. There are areas of stony soil, ground in which the good seed of God's Word has been dropped. It germinates, flourishes briefly, comes up against rocks of resistance, then withers away to nothing.

Any point or any place in life where a person prefers to disobey God, to go his own way and do his own thing is stony soil. This is what it means to have a hard heart. It is the kind of ground where the good gardener encounters enormous grief and labor to get anything to grow.

Those areas in which we stubbornly refuse to comply with Christ's commands are barren, boulder-strewn soil. We block the movement of His Spirit in our affairs, hindering the action of His Word. There is no growth. Nothing happens. Our souls are impoverished and our lives languish. And there is no ongoing growth that will produce fruit.

By His Gracious Spirit, God wants to clear the stony, stubborn soil of our souls. He wants to plant the trees of His own righteousness in every spot from which a stone of disobedience has been dug. Our Divine Gardener wants to cultivate a gorgeous garden where before there were only barren boulders of bald resistance to His Word.

If this is to happen we must want it to take place. By faith in Christ we must believe that He actually can take the waste land of our lives and transform it into a garden of God. We must ask Him to give us a vision, a preview, a glimpse of what He can do with a hard heart, a stony will, a stubborn and wayward disposition. Perhaps He will show us the miracle of transformation He has performed in another person's character.

This is basically what happened to me as a teenager. My earliest childhood impressions of my Dad were of a tough, demanding man. He was hard with himself, hard on others, and difficult for God to handle. But as the years rolled by, the Lord in His own persistent, powerful way was clearing the stony ground in my father's life, just as he himself was removing the boulders from his own hillside acres.

The result was that throughout my teens I watched, awestruck, the transformation that took place in Dad's character. Gradually, surely and steadily he mellowed into one of the most lovable men I ever met. He became gracious, gentle, forbearing and thoughtful. His entire life was fragrant with the fully ripened fruitage of God's Spirit.

If in truth we want such a change of character

it can take place. We will earnestly and honestly determine to do God's will, setting ourselves to comply with Christ's commands. Attuning ourselves to be sensitive to His Spirit as He speaks to us through His Word, we will take time to meditate over the Scriptures. We will take them seriously and will respond to the call of Christ. We will allow ourselves to be open and available to the inner working of God Himself. And we will be amazed at our growth in godliness.

"For it is God who worketh in you both to will and to do of his good pleasure" (Phil. 2:13).

The third type of rocky soil is what is known as gravelly ground. It is land interlaced with layers of gravel or streaks of sand. Frequently a thin cover of top soil conceals the true condition of the ground beneath the surface.

Seeds or plants that take root here will generally spring up swiftly. They show rather sudden, spectacular growth, but a few days of hot sun and wind soon wipe them out as they wither away. The substrata of sand and gravel is like a sieve through which all the moisture and nutrients drain away. Roots shrivel and die. And only desolation remains.

Our Lord had often seen fields of this sort. They were common on the ridges and slopes of marginal land that often left their owners impoverished. He said some of us were like that gravelly ground. Little or nothing would grow there successfully.

What is the parallel in our personal lives?

There are two.

The gravel layer that lies below the surface with

so many of us is the ground of our *ingratitude.* It is the deeply ingrained grumbling in which so many of us indulge. We complain against God for the way in which He handles our lives and arranges our circumstances. Peevishly we protest our lot in life, finding fault with the way He leads us and the places He puts us.

Of course most people do not proclaim their petty grievances in public hearing. Quite the opposite. Most prefer to put on a fine front. They pretend that all is well behind their false façade. But deep beneath the surface of their superficial smiles lie hard, resistant, sometimes defiant attitudes of resentment toward God's arrangement of their affairs.

This is absolutely fatal to any sort of Christian growth. It grieves God's Gracious Spirit. In fact, He simply cannot produce His fruit in such grumbling, gravelly ground. In Hebrews 3:12–19 we are warned solemnly not to harden ourselves against God by complaining. This is what the nation of Israel did when delivered from Egypt. It provoked God to great anger.

The streak of sand in our experience is the habit of fault-finding, criticism, and censure of others. Unless we are alerted to this, it can easily become a chronic condition. We can develop a *mind-set* that habitually sees only the dark, difficult side of life. Conditioned and accustomed to hard attitudes of condemnation that invariably put other people in a bad light, we become tough, demanding, and abrasive. This is not good ground in which the Divine Gardener can grow His sunny fruits.

He comes to us and urges upon us several steps for dealing with our grumbling against God and our faultfinding with others.

Instead of raging against the Lord for the way He manages our lives, let us carefully consider all the benefits He bestows. Take a piece of paper; sit down alone in a quiet spot; write down one by one all the good things—the delights and pleasures He has made possible for you. List everything—the sound of music; the laughter of children; the sunrise; the scent of a rose; the clasp of a friend's hand; the loyalty of a dog. If one is honest, there is no end to the list. It is an exercise that will break our grumbling, pulverize our pride and humble our hard hearts before a gracious God.

Look for and deliberately seek out the lovely, beautiful, noble, honest, and gracious aspects of life. Search for the best in others. We are told pointedly to do this in Philippians 4.

Lastly use the three great words that spell out growth in godliness.

1. Acknowledge—"O God, You are very God. You know exactly what You are doing with me. It is for my best. All is well."

2. Accept His Management. Herein lies peace and rest. No longer will I resist or resent Your work in my life. You are the Good Gardener.

3. Approve of Christ's Arrangement of Your Affairs. It is Your intention I should become fruitful. Under Your good hand this will happen. Thanks for everything.

This will turn pouting into praise—grumbling into

gratitude. It is the key to releasing all the energies of God the Holy Spirit to move fully and freely through my daily life. He will do exceedingly more than I can ever ask or think (Eph. 3:19–21).

THREE

Thorny People, Lost in the Weeds

The third type of soil which Our Lord referred to as being *nonproductive* was thorny ground. Such ground was infested with weeds and thistles. Any garden riddled and choked with noxious plants simply was incapable of fruit production.

Because of its diverse topography and terrain, some of it semidesert, Palestine was notorious for its wide variety of thorns, thistles and briers. Over 200 species of undesirable weeds invaded cultivated land to compete with the crops planted with such painstaking care. It was a never-ending struggle to grow good gardens and keep fields free of foreign plants.

Both in the Old Testament Hebrew text and the New Testament Greek some seventeen different words are used to describe this undesirable, thorny sort of growth. In the English language a variety of words are likewise used to translate the meaning. We find such nouns as *thorns, thistles, briers, brambles,* and so on appearing in the scriptural account.

Always, the picture portrayed in connection with gardening or farming is that of the enormous problems posed by the growth of these undesirable plants. Jesus was very familiar with the people's struggle to produce a harvest of fruit or grain in the face of competition from thistles and thorns in their crops.

He used pointed parables to illustrate this fact. In His mighty Sermon on the Mount, He asked the point-blank question, "Do men gather grapes of thorns, or figs of thistles?" (Matt. 7:16). If one's vineyard was choked with brambles, he did not look for a bumper crop of grapes. It was a straightforward case of one or the other.

Brambles and briers, thorns and thistles had the nasty capacity to so crowd and choke the grower's planting that the crop was utterly smothered and stifled. There was virtually *no production—no fruitage.*

Our Lord made the point that some of our lives were just like that. They were so infested with noxious weeds that there could be no harvest.

Unlike our modern agricultural techniques where all sorts of selective herbicides are used to control weeds in crops, primitive people had only one remedy—clean cultivation of the ground. And this was a well-nigh impossible task. Thistle seeds could be blown in on the wind from miles away. Wild birds that had fed on berries and brambles could drop their dung on any garden depositing foreign seeds in their droppings. Wild animals and domestic beasts could carry all sorts of burrs and weed seeds in their coats across the countryside.

So there was no such thing as an eternally clean garden. It was only the owner's constant diligence and care that could guarantee a beautiful and productive piece of ground. And often even then, in spite of his most persistent efforts, the invaders would be present to prevent full fruitage.

Jesus likened some of us to this sort of weed-infested soil. He declared very forthrightly that such a garden was simply *unfruitful.*

The question which we must therefore ask ourselves is solemn and searching. *"What is growing in the Ground of my life?"*

Putting it another way we might ask, "What takes up the most space in my life? What occupies most of my time and attention? What has gained prime place in my priorities? What has become the chief outgrowth and production in the overall performance of my life? What is the net result of my living—worthless weeds or fine fruit of eternal value?"

Christ made it clear that there were three types of weeds:

1) The cares, anxieties, worries or interests of this world.

2) The deceitfulness of wealth; the attraction of affluence.

3) The covetousness for things; the magnetism of materialism.

Because of the intense competition from some of

these influences, our lives are total crop failures. The good seed of God's Word implanted in us by His Gracious Spirit simply comes to nothing. It is simply smothered by fierce and formidable competition from foreign ideals. Of these the first Jesus named would appear to be the least dangerous.

1. Worldly Cares

Like death and taxes, the cares of living are just an integral part of the very warp and woof of life. We delude ourselves if we believe that somehow the children of God are exempt from the stresses and strains of the human family.

Those preachers and teachers who would lead us to think that a Christian's life can be a trouble-free trip do us all a great disservice. It simply is not so. The Word of God makes it abundantly apparent that "many are the afflictions of the righteous" (Ps. 34:19). Our Lord declared flatly, "In this world ye shall have tribulation—but be of good cheer, I have overcome the world" (John 16:33).

All of us, without exception, have laid upon us the responsibility to earn a proper and appropriate living. Whatever our lot in life may be, we are instructed to work diligently and heartily. We are taught to provide adequately for our families, and we are told to pay our taxes, to meet our moral obligations as law-abiding people. We have clearly defined guidelines laid down in God's Word as to what our behavior should be in the human community of which we are an integral part.

It follows, therefore, that life does make definite demands upon us. If we are to live well-rounded, balanced, fruitful lives we must meet the responsibilities placed upon us by both God and man. How do we do this? How do we avoid becoming eccentric ascetics who desire to withdraw entirely from the challenge of society? How do we keep from engrossing ourselves in the world so that we become engulfed and smothered by its deceptive and destructive philosophies or ideologies?

Our Lord dealt with this dilemma in great detail in His majestic Sermon on the Mount in Matthew 6. There He reassures our questing hearts that our Heavenly Father does know the needs and demands laid upon us by life. He knows we require food, shelter, drink, and clothing. Since He provides adequately for birds and lilies, He likewise provides for His people upon the planet.

The crux of the issue is my preoccupation with those cares which press in upon me. Do I really believe that my Heavenly Father, if I trust Him fully, will care for me? Where are my priorities in the picture? Is the focus of my attention upon earning my living by the sweat of my own endeavors—or is it upon the trustworthiness of God?

As a word of personal witness to the reliability of the Lord I would like to share my own experience here. Up until I was nearly forty I worried incessantly about making a living, providing for my family, success in my endeavors, security for the future. And even when all of these were taken care of my dear wife would say, "Phillip, even if you haven't anything to worry about you will soon invent something to fret over."

It was at that advanced age in life, through a most traumatic experience, which I shall not describe here, I was virtually stripped of all I had struggled to secure. In total abandon and trembling, childlike faith I flung myself upon the care and commitments of my Heavenly Father. The past twenty years have been a most powerful demonstration of His willingness to provide in a remarkable manner for my every need in all areas of my life. This is not to boast but to give hearty thanks for His total trustworthiness.

It is a straightforward question of priorities. The instant an individual determines to put Christ at the center of his life, to give Him the place of priority and consideration, he is out of the woods. He is no longer lost among the weeds of worry and concern. The ground of his being is cleared of the confusing entanglements of his contemporaries. There is now time and space to produce fruit for God of eternal consequence.

A second aspect which we need to discover in this dilemma of worldly cares is the time factor. Christ emphasized strongly that each day did have its difficulties. "Sufficient unto the day is the evil thereof" (Matt. 6:34).

We cannot afford to drag the distress of either yesterday or tomorrow into today. I cannot allow myself to "borrow sorrow from tomorrow." I must not permit the sure joy of this day to be jeopardized

by the uncertainties of the future or the empty re-
grets of the past.

In very truth I have only today. Yesterday is gone
forever. There is no guarantee I shall be here tomorrow. So in reality I am locked into a single *day-tight*
time and space concept. I have the choice—either
I can worry my way through it or I can revel
and rejoice in this interval of time provided by my
Father.

One of my favorite phrases is, "Relish the moment." This is the day the Lord has arranged for
me so I will rejoice and delight in it (See Ps. 118:24).

Living in this attitude of carefree goodwill frees
our spirits from the stress and tension of worldly
cares. Like the continual cultivation of a garden to
keep it clear of weed growth, so this daily discipline
of delighting in God's faithful provision for us is a
soul-liberating process.

As I live this way the ever present would-be weeds
of worry, anxiety, and preoccupation with petty concerns wither away. They cease to dominate my days.
Instead, I become engrossed with the great and joy-
ous purposes of God for both the planet and His
people. My focus is transferred from my needs to
those of others. In all of this there is abundant opportunity to be productive, helpful, and great-hearted.
In the Master Gardener's hands, even my most humble endeavors become fruitful beyond my wildest
dreams.

The third way to clear the weeds of worry from
our lives is best summed up in the simple little

rhyme: "I'll give God my best; He will do the rest!"

Whatever life gives us opportunity to do, let us do it well. Let us do it to the best of our ability, then leave the results with Christ.

It is not for us to decide or determine what the net result of our living will be. It is God who keeps the eternal accounts. Only He can ascertain that which is of consequence in His economy.

Yet we rejoice over each day we can live for Him. We give hearty and humble thanks for His abundant and gracious care, living in a constant "attitude of gratitude." To live this way is to live out in the open sunlight of His presence; it is to live in honest dignity and strength; it is to live in serene simplicity; it is to live above the clutter and complications of a complex society that would crowd and choke out our fruitfulness for God.

2. The Deceitfulness of Wealth

Some Christians have a distinct misunderstanding about wealth. Wealth in itself is not wrong. Riches are not necessarily evil. Affluence is not always a sin. Immense finances are not invariably wicked.

If so, then God would certainly never have bestowed wealth on men like Abraham, Joseph, Solomon, Job or Hezekiah . . . not to mention some modern-day heroes of the faith.

The difficulty lies in our attitude toward wealth. How is it dispensed? For what purposes is it accumulated? To what ends is it dedicated?

For most people the dilemma is the deceitfulness

of riches. Riches have the capacity to distort our thinking; riches may blind us to eternal values; riches also have the insidious ability to dominate our desires.

By its very nature wealth leads us to put our trust in it rather than in the One who gave us the ability to accumulate it. Riches have a subtle way of suggesting to us that they themselves can provide security and serenity. In very truth they do just the opposite.

I have found that very often the richest and most wealthy people are also among the least secure and serene. They fret endlessly over the possibility of losing their wealth. This leads to endless worry, anxiety, and discontent.

Many very wealthy people, if not preoccupied with losing their wealth, are equally exercised about increasing it. It is not enough to own one car—we need two! One home is not enough. We need a summer house as well. It is not enough to have one million dollars. Two or even three are better. So there really is no end to the continuous scramble.

Jesus knew all about this. He told parables to point out the folly of pursuing the pot of gold at the end of the rainbow. It was a pointless, pathetic, fruitless pursuit. Remember the rich farmer who determined to build ever larger and better barns to hold his bumper crops? He ended up a pauper who had never established any credit with God. He had no eternal crop of lasting value in God's economy. All his frantic efforts had terminated in fruitlessness as far as God was concerned. He was a fool who had been deceived by his own insatiable desire for wealth. His had been a weedy life, lost in the jungle growth of "getting, getting, getting."

The world's philosophy is "What can I get out of life?" In blazing contrast Christ comes along with the clear, clean, cutting command: "Give what you can to your generation!"

To follow the one is to become entangled in the undergrowth of selfish, self-centered living. To follow Christ is to have the ground of our lives cleared of the constricting weeds that would wrap themselves around us in our pursuit of wealth for its own sake.

Obviously we cannot devote our days to nothing but making money and at the same time devote them to serving God.

The question comes down to this: "Is wealth my master or is Christ?" Who controls what?

For the child of God there is only one way to go in this area. Any riches that come to me are a trust from the Lord. They are not mine to invest, use or squander recklessly. I have no right ever to claim that I am a self-made person. That is colossal conceit and an affront to God. Every capacity, ability to think, strength to work, and means to accumulate wealth comes from Him as a gift. Therefore in humility and simplicity I assume stewardship for all that He entrusts to me. I use it sparingly and wisely to meet my own needs, generously and graciously to minister to the needs of others.

To handle wealth this way is to be a fruitful garden for God. To use it any other way is to allow my outlook, thinking, and behavior to be choked up with the crass commercialism of a godless society. Ultimately in so doing I shall lose my own soul and there will be no fruit for the Great Good Gardener.

In passing let it be said, especially for young people, that if God finds you to be trustworthy in small things at first, He will quickly entrust you with greater riches. Few are the men and women to whom God can give great wealth. It too often goes to their heads. They don't know how to handle it. But those who do can use riches and wealth in mighty ways to produce abundant fruit for the Lord.

It is they who clothe the naked, feed the hungry, heal the sick, educate the illiterate, bring the good news to the lost, cheer the weary, and heal the hurts of a sick and suffering world.

"In as much as ye have done it unto one of the least of these my brethren, ye have done it unto me" (Matt. 25:40).

3. The Magnetism of Materialism

Jesus put it bluntly: "The lusts of other things entering in, choke the word, and it becometh unfruitful" (Mark 4:19).

As with wealth so with *things*—many of them in themselves are neither wrong nor wicked. It is the desire for and determined drive to attain wealth which so often divert us from the more important eternal, divine values in life.

We settle for second best.

We are occupied with tinsel while we could be reaching for the stars.

Having grown up overseas in a frugal family and a humble home, I was trained to live in a rather spartan manner. I have yet to adapt myself to the affluence and luxury of North America. All during my formative years I lived among Africans who existed on very little. Their possessions were minimal, their wants remarkably few, and yet their contentment, good will and gay laughter were contagious. Amidst their simplicity and what we in the West would consider stern austerity, I learned first-hand the very basic truth of our Lord's remarks in this area: "Take heed, and beware of covetousness; for a man's life consisteth not in the abundance of the things which he possesseth" (Luke 12:15).

Yet everything in our culture cries out against this concept. Western civilization is based no longer upon the great verities in the Word of God. It simply is not true to say now "We trust in God." Rather our whole society has shifted its weight and reliance upon the twin pillars of the productivity of its industry and the purchasing power of its people.

This is why we face imminent disaster.

Never in human history has any civilization used its mind, strength, and genius to invent, manufacture, and market such a multiplicity of *things*. I am basically a person of simple wants. The array of gadgets, gimmicks, and gaudy displays in our large stores quite literally frightens me. Such a plethora of extravagance makes me uneasy. The endless array of food, clothing, furniture, hardware, textiles, and other items that flood from our factories leave me ill at ease. All I want is to get outside the stores into the sunshine and fresh air. I don't need ten thousand different items to lend dignity to my life or happiness to my home.

But our culture is not content to leave me alone in my simple life style. Day and night the mass media, magazines, newspapers, books, billboards, and flyers crammed into my bulging mail box scream at me to buy this, strive for that, acquire something here, come to possess something there. Relentlessly pressure is applied, both in bold, blatant ways and in smooth, subtle, sophisticated sales pitches to cause me to purchase more than I really need, all much beyond my means.

Those born and raised in this culture are of course completely conditioned to it. They accept this vaunted way of life, built around things, to be the best in the world.

Combined with all of this is the entire credit system. It enables a person, with nothing more than his name on a piece of paper, to purchase almost anything he or she may desire. From boots to Buicks you can buy what your heart desires even if it does plunge you so deep in debt that it may take you twenty years to recover.

The net result of all this *in-put* into our lives is that most of us are irrevocably preoccupied with the magnetism of materialism. We are not only totally mesmerized by the attraction of things, we are snared and engulfed in the difficulties of discharging our debts to pay for them. As if that were not enough we later discover that they contribute virtually nothing to the sum total of human happiness, but more often turn out to be an absolute headache. We do not possess them, they possess us. We are enslaved and trapped into the treadmill of an economy based on appalling waste and obsolescence.

Our Lord said emphatically that it was this sort of *in-put* that would choke out His good Word in the gentle garden of our lives.

Against the garrulous demands of our consumer-oriented society, God's Word sometimes seems absurd. The world urges us to "get, get, get." Christ comes along and says, "Give, give, give." The world says happiness lies in everything from sex to spaghetti. Christ comes along and says our serenity is in knowing Him. The world says make a big splash and show your success by your possessions—impress people. Christ comes along and says that the greatest amongst us is the one who is willing and ready to be a servant.

Who has truth? Where is the answer? Can we really be fruitful and productive for God amid all the pressures put upon us? Or are we going to let the insidious ideologies, the crass concepts of commercialism invade our lives like weed seeds blown into a carefully cultivated piece of ground? Are we going to permit the false philosophies of a humanistic society to choke out the crop of eternal values which God by His Spirit wishes to produce in our experience?

Where is my heart? In things or in Christ?

Where are my affections? On possessions or on God?

Where are my priorities? In covetousness or in cooperation with the compelling overtures of God's Gracious Spirit?

To what refrains does my soul respond? To the clamor of my contemporary world or to the call of Christ the Good Gardener?

I know of only two ways in which we can be turned away from the tyranny of our times, the vicious, victimizing obsession with *things*. Here they are. They will clear the ground of our lives from the weeds of human deception quicker than anything else.

1) God made man for *Himself*, to be His child. He created us with the incredible capacity not only to commune with Him, but to know Him intimately—to be His companions, conformed to His very character.

Anyone who devotes his life, time, and attention to any lesser thing, no matter how grand or noble or glamorous, has missed the mark and the whole purpose of living.

To allow myself to be encumbered and enslaved by things is to have the whole ground of my being cluttered and choked with transient values—whereas I could be producing fruit of eternal duration and consequences. A poor exchange indeed.

2) It is only as I respond promptly and positively to the claims of Christ upon my life and character that I will discover He alone has truth. He alone

holds the secret of serenity—strength and stability in a shaky society.

It is in the face of the expulsive power of this new found affection for Him that the attraction and magnetism of materialism will wane. Then the ground of my garden will be free of weeds to allow Him to produce therein His own beautiful fruit.

FOUR

Productive People, Good Ground

In bold and dramatic contrast to the three types of unfruitful, nonproductive soils, Jesus depicted a piece of good ground. He said that when good seed was sown on good soil there could be a flourishing garden full of fruit.

In some instances the returns would be thirty, sixty or even one hundred times that which was originally planted. This was genuine productivity and it was the sort of return the gardener fully expected from his labor on the land.

It is important to recognize the basic fact that rocky soils, weed-infested ground, and land lost to pathways were considered *nonproductive*. They were simply incapable of growing a crop in their natural condition. It was not a question of being somewhat or partially fruitful. There was *nothing*. It was lost ground. There was no crop.

Only the painstaking labor and loving care of a diligent owner could alter their condition. It required tremendous toil with teams and tools to break up hard ground; to clear stony soil; to cultivate and clean up weed-choked land.

The hardened clay clods, set like cement under passing feet, had to be pulverized with plows and harrows and hoes. The rock-riddled ground had to be cleared, the stones carted away to make room for the crop. The roots and stumps of thorny growth had to be torn from the soil and the weed growth piled and burned to fit the garden for the seed. It all required a tremendous amount of toil to turn a piece of untamed, untilled land into good ground for a garden. *Even the best of soil must first be broken before it can become beautiful.*

Only yesterday afternoon, in the mellow warmth of a late September afternoon, I began to prepare a piece of garden soil on a wild, untamed chunk of virgin land that has never grown anything but wild brambles and the hated knapweed. No shovel had ever penetrated this ground before. And as I worked the sweat streamed from my back.

The labor I was engaged in was a labor of love. I love the soil. I am a man close to the land. One of the great delights of my long and adventurous life has been to take marginal soils, whether in great sweeping acreages on large ranches or on little garden plots, and bring them into a state of maximum productivity. This demands hard work and skill.

But it is deeply rewarding and tremendously exciting.

Yesterday the piece of ground on which I began work was probably the least promising corner of my whole property that lies beside a lovely lake. It was choked with weeds. Gnarled granite boulders jutted up here and there through its surface soil. It was riddled with the tangled roots of old wild rose bushes and tough greasewood that had grown there unchecked. For untold years it had been tramped hard where people had hiked across it.

In spite of all these defects and disadvantages I began to dig. I dug with joy and hope. I dug with a song in my spirit, for I could see beyond the boulders, the weeds, the roots, and the hard crusted ground. I could see a garden flourishing there the following spring.

The perspiration poured from me into the warm autumn sun. My muscles heaved and strained as I turned the tough sod. It took tremendous tugs to tear some of the wild roots from the ground. Soon I had a large pile of them ready to burn. Again and again my shovel struck rock. From this small patch of ground I hauled away wheelbarrow loads of stones. Mounds of accumulated debris had to be dug away.

When I was through for the day I smiled. For a good piece of ground, carefully husbanded, lay smooth and dark and soft and clean ready to be sown next spring. There would burst from this warm earth a rich array of green plants that would produce basketfuls of fruit and vegetables next summer.

There would be more than enough bounty to feed ourselves and our friends.

This is what God, the Great, Good Gardener has to do in our lives. We are not naturally "good ground." Beyond our hardness and perverseness He sees the potential locked up in our stony souls. He works on us in hope and love.

None of us is too tough for Him to tackle. In spite of our perverseness, pride, and pollution He can transform us from a wasteland to a well-watered garden. We should want it that way. It does not come easily. It does not happen in a single day. The digging, the clearing, the cultivation may seem to us to be devastating; the disciplining of our souls may seem severe. Yet afterwards it produces the peaceable fruits of His own planting (see Heb. 12:10, 11).

Too many of us as Christians are content to remain wild, waste land. We much prefer to stay untouched by God's good hand. In fact we are frightened of having our little lives turned over by the deep work of His convicting Spirit. We don't want the shearing, cutting, powerful thrust of His Word to lay us open to the sunlight of His own presence. We prefer to remain weedy ground and stony soil—or pathetic pathway people.

We delude ourselves into thinking that out of our old unchanged characters and dispositions somehow a good crop is coming forth. It simply cannot be. You simply do not gather grapes from a thistle patch nor figs from wild brambles. And the good gardener does not even come there looking for fruit. It is strictly a *no-crop* condition. It is a total loss to both ourselves and God.

Our Lord was very specific in describing the spiritual aspects of productive people. Here they are stated in His own words.

1) They are people who bear His Word and all that it implies.

2) They are people who receive and accept that Word.

3) They are people whose lives because of that Word produce the fruit of God's Gracious Spirit in their characters, conduct, and conversation.

This being the case we should carefully examine each of these aspects to understand exactly what Christ meant. The first is *hearing the Word.*

During the days of His earthly sojourn among men, one of the greatest distresses to our Lord was this question of people "hearing" His Word. Over and over He reiterated the fact that "Ears ye have but ye hear not." Or couching the same sentiment in another way He would insist that "hearing" had to be linked with "doing." It was not enough merely to be exposed to truth. There simply had to be a positive response on the part of the hearer.

There are three definite, deliberate steps involved in "hearing" God's Word in order for it to become effective and fruitful. Here they are:

1) I must recognize it is God who is speaking. Unless His Word is held in great respect as being of divine content I will simply equate it with other men's words.

Only when I reach the point where I solemnly place great store upon what He says will it ever become a powerful force in my life.

Only when I really take Him seriously will His Word be made Spirit and life (supernatural life) to me.

Only when I recognize that what I am hearing is in fact and in truth divine revelation designed by deity for my own good, will I hear it as a word from above.

God has chosen to articulate Himself to me as a man in four ways: Through the natural created universe around me; through His Word expressed by inspired men who reported it in human language I can read and understand; through the person of Jesus Christ, the Word made flesh, exemplified in human form; through those other humble men and women in whom He deigns to reside by His own Gracious Spirit.

He may speak to me deliberately and distinctly through any one or all of these ways. It is my responsibility then to recognize: "O God, You are communicating with me. I will listen. I do recognize Your voice communing with me."

2) Secondly, to hear His Word implies essentially that *I must respond to it in a positive way.*

In other words I must alert myself to act on it.

I must set aside whatever else preoccupies my thoughts and give my undivided attention to the Lord.

It is not good enough to "half listen" to God. He demands my total concentration on what He is conveying to me. He knows that anything less will leave me half-hearted.

Unless this happens the seed of that Word is simply snatched away by the birds. I don't really believe it. It has fallen on stony soil. Or I am too caught up with other concerns, so it is smothered out.

3) The third step in "hearing" God speak implies that promptly and swiftly *I shall run to do what He requests.*

My positive response results in immediate action on my part. His will is done. His wishes are carried out His desires are complied with happily. His commands are executed without delay or debate.

In short I simply do what He asks me to do.

This is faith in action—the faith of obedience.

This is the gateway into the good ground of God's garden.

This is to "hear" the Word and have it come alive.

This is to have Him implant the good seed of His good intentions for me in the good, warm, open, prepared soil of my responsive soul.

The seed will germinate. The young plants will prosper and grow vigorously. There will be fruit production of His choosing—a harvest that delights Him and refreshes others.

The second striking characteristic of good ground, according to Jesus, was that *it received the word.*

The word "receive" is one of the terms we glibly bandy about in Christian circles without stopping to discover what it really means. We speak of "receiving" Christ, "receiving" the gifts of the Spirit, "receiving" forgiveness. In just the same way we talk freely about "accepting" Christ or "accepting" our salvation without really understanding its full implications and responsibilities.

All too often to "receive" or "accept" are merely thought of in terms of taking from the hand of another that which is offered as a gift.

But to receive or accept in a spiritual sense goes far beyond this limited view.

First of all it means that I must be open, receptive, and amenable to God and His Word.

There cannot be either reluctance or resistance on my part.

It implies that my mind, emotions, disposition, and spirit are open—that I am indeed friable soil prepared by the deep, diligent *in-working* of God's Spirit, ready to receive and accept the seed of His Word introduced to me.

If I am a person with a closed mind, with strong personal prejudices, with deep difficult doubts, with bigoted presuppositions about eternal verities, quite obviously I am not ready to receive divine truth. His Word in me will come to nothing. It will be wasted on the birds of unbelief, on rocky resentment, and on the weeds of worldliness.

So to receive God's Word means I must welcome it. I must reach out to take and accept it eagerly—ready to literally assimilate and incorporate it into the very soil of my daily experience.

It is not some peculiar philosophy relegated to religious ritual once or twice a week. Rather, that

70

viable, vital word is something that must spring to life as it germinates in the good soil of my daily experiences with Christ.

The whole idea of "receiving" God's Word is also associated with my total availability to it. The whole ground of my life needs to be reachable.

In a good garden there are no spots still littered with stones. There are no odd corners cluttered and choked out with weeds. There are no beaten paths where nothing at all can grow. All the ground has to be tilled. All the soil must finally be fitted for fruitfulness.

It will take time to do this. But it must be done. The Spirit of God is very persistent. The Good Gardener must have full management. Christ comes to take over every area made arable.

The extent to which a piece of good ground has received and responded to good sowing is eventually demonstrated by how little soil shows. The entire area planted will be taken over, covered and smothered in a luxuriance of green growth. The onlooker will see, not the soil, but the bountiful produce on it.

So with our lives. If in truth we have received the good Word, and the very life of Christ flourishes, it is the fruitage of His character, the fragrance of His conduct that will be evident to those around us.

It is proper and appropriate in a book of this sort to pause here briefly and explain in simple language exactly what it means to receive Christ. For He was and is "The Word Incarnate" i.e. "The Word of God very God made manifest, expressed visibly and audibly in human form."

The beloved, aged John, writing in the twilight of his life declared emphatically: "He came unto his own, and his own received him not. But as many as received him, to them gave he power to become the Sons of God . . ." (John 1:11, 12).

From the cataclysmic point in human history when Adam the federal head of the human family flatly refused to comply with God's best intentions for him, all men have been contaminated with self-will that leads to sin. In spite of the pride, perverseness, and pollution of people that results from sin and selfish self-centeredness God has come to seek and to save and to reconcile wayward lost men and women to Himself.

Because man's best efforts to reclaim and restore himself in the presence of an incredibly holy, righteous, and loving God fall far short, he is incapable of his own redemption. God Himself had to intervene on our behalf. He chose to become the supreme Substitute, who alone could atone for our misconduct and expiate for our sins.

This He did in the person of His own Son, Jesus Christ, the Savior of the world. He is *the Word, the very visible expression of the invisible God.* This "God in the flesh" came to live, move, serve, and die amongst us—to be resurrected and return to His former glory.

The "perfect doing" and the "perfect dying" of God in Christ, because it was that of the *Infinite One Himself,* suffices for all men of all time, be there billions upon billions of human beings.

The good news of our salvation, our forgiveness, our acceptance with God is that He Himself, in Christ, has done all that is necessary to deliver us from the dilemma of our sins and self-will. Through His shed blood, broken body, and complete sacrifice on our behalf He has paid the price for our perverseness, pride, and pollution. It matters not in what area of our lives we may have sinned.

At Calvary He who was God, very God died for us *physically* to atone for sins done in the flesh; He died morally, being made sin for us who knew no sin, in order that we might be made right with His righteousness *morally;* He died *spiritually* in total separation from His Father, which was to taste the awfulness of hell itself, to atone for our spiritual wrongdoing and heal our separation from a loving God.

It is on the basis of this titanic transaction, beyond the capacity of any man to fully plumb, that we are invited to *receive Him as divine royalty. We are urged to accept Him as the only way of reconciling ourselves to a loving God. We receive Him as our Savior.*

This is the supreme objective work of God done on our behalf for our justification in His presence. He has acted for us in history. He asks us to receive, to welcome, to take to ourselves, to believe in and trust this Living Christ who has given Himself to us through His death that we might live through His righteousness. Through His generosity there is *imputed* (credited to our account) His righteousness.

Yet God does not leave it at that. He actually comes now, in the present moment, and invites us to also *receive Him as divine royalty by His Spirit.* He God, very God in Christ, by His Gracious Spirit approaches us asking for the privilege to actually enter our lives as a Royal Resident.

"Behold, I stand at the door, and knock: if any man *hear* my voice, and open the door, I will come in to him, and will sup with him (share life with him), and he with me" (Rev. 3:20).

The person who so receives, accepts or invites Christ by His Spirit into his life, must of necessity also recognize Him as *Lord of his life, and receive Him as Sovereign.*

It is the Sovereign Spirit of the living God resident in our lives who does His supreme subjective work of remaking us. It is He who renews and re-creates us. This is the whole basis of our rebirth and sanctification before God. It is His joy and delight to conform us to Christ. He, the Gracious Gardener, does the deep work to produce and reproduce within our lives the fruits and attributes of His own character.

It was to this profound process that our Lord referred when He said that the third aspect of good ground was, *it brings forth fruit.*

That is to say there is reproduction. God actually duplicates in human character the attributes of His own person. For example, He is known as the God of all mercy. Therefore it follows that in due time mercy will become a hallmark of the man or woman in whom He resides and is at work.

We are told quite emphatically, for instance, that the good seed of the very love (selflessness) of God is shed abroad (scattered throughout) our hearts by the Holy Spirit who is given to us (see Rom. 5:5). Therefore it is proper and legitimate for us to look for that sort of selfless, self-giving to spring up and become apparent in the Christian's life.

It is important to note, too, that God Himself comes looking for that love to be an integral part of our character. As was stated emphatically earlier in this book the chief criteria by which either God or men can conclude whether or not we truly are Christians is by our fruits. The basis upon which we can obtain empirical evidence that a person truly believes in Christ and has received Him both as Savior and Lord is by the fruit of God's own character reproduced in that life. There simply has to be something of the likeness of Christ apparent as proof positive that God is actually at work within.

A skeptical society so often charges the church with hypocrisy for this very reason. They look for attributes of character and attitudes of behavior that are Godlike in those who claim to be Christians. If these are lacking they quite naturally and legitimately insist the churchgoer is a phony and a fake.

This is why our Lord was so devastating in His denunciation of the scribes, Pharisees, and Sadducees of His day. They pretended to be so pious. Yet within they were rotten with corruption, greed, and pride. Their lives were a pretense. They were not good ground. There were no fruits of godliness. Jesus declared emphatically to Nicodemus, the pious Pharisee: "You simply have to be born again—re-made and re-worked."

In Part II of this book each of the fruits of God's

own character will be examined carefully. We will see how each is expressed in His conduct toward us, and we will see its effect in our own lives—in our relationship to others as well as back to God Himself. And we will study the means and methods God employs to produce each fruit in our lives.

But before we do that it is essential to emphasize here that the one great, essential ingredient for good soil to be productive under God's good hand is obedience or responsiveness. In our permissive, rather lawless and undisciplined society it is not popular to discuss obedience. Most people prefer to do their own thing, live their own lives, go their own way.

This is selfish self-centeredness at its worst.

Such an attitude is absolutely fatal to fruitfulness.

It is the sure recipe for barrenness, and its end result is desolation and despair.

Note that God's Gracious Spirit is given only to those who obey (Acts 5:32). He will not enter nor reside where there is rebellion or resentment against His Royal Presence. He who is sovereign seeks for, expects, and counts on our complete cooperation and compliance with His commands in all areas of our lives.

If we truly love Christ and love God we will not only endeavor, but also deeply desire to carry out His wishes and will for us. Read John 14 and 15 to verify this.

Five minutes of implicit obedience to God at any point will generate more fruits of right living in our experience than five years of theological or doctrinal discussion that end only in dilly-dallying with the truth.

As God by His Spirit reveals new areas of my life into which He wishes to move and work, my responsibility is to allow Him to have His way without resistance or hindrance. As He steadily and surely takes over more and more ground in my daily experience the crop yield will gradually increase from 30- to 60- to 100-fold.

The more good ground of obedient behavior He encounters and cultivates the greater the productivity. There can be a bountiful harvest of divine fruit because of the Good Gardener's great skill and my simple, humble, hearty response to His work within.

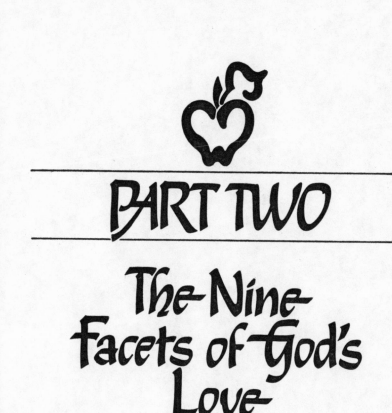

PART TWO

The Nine Facets of God's Love

FIVE

Love—
the Life
of God

So much has been written about the love of God that one almost hesitates to discuss the subject again. Some of God's great and noble saints have applied themselves so diligently to a study of this concept that it would seem all that can be said has already been reported for us. Amongst these writings perhaps the most winsome and powerful is Henry Drummond's *The Greatest Thing in the World.*

Any person who will earnestly, prayerfully read that essay once a week, every week, for three months is bound to have the entire fabric of his/her character colored and changed by God's Gracious Spirit.

Love—the First Fruit

Notwithstanding all that has already been preached and published about God's love it must

81

be examined here. It is the first and foremost of the fruits of God's Spirit. It is much, much more than merely "one of the fruits." In reality it is the very basic, essential life of the living Christ which expresses itself in all the nine fruits enumerated both in Galatians 5:22, 23 and 1 Corinthians 13:1–7.

The love of God is the very life of God.

That life, if allowed to grow freely in the good ground of the well prepared soil of our souls, will flourish and fructify in various ways. It will not always express itself in exactly the same manner or to the same degree. Each of us differs in our display of divine life. Yet the evidence of deity *within* is demonstrated irrevocably by supernatural fruit *without.*

Such fruit can and does come only from above.

It is not something which we can counterfeit.

The very life of God, epitomized in the love of God, originates only and always with Him.

Like good seed introduced into good garden soil, it must come from a source outside the garden. It does not, nor can it ever spring from the soil of our own souls and spirits spontaneously.

There may be theologians, scholars, and teachers who would try to tell us that there is inherent good in man which if properly tended and cultivated can be gradually improved so that it ultimately becomes divine. This may strongly appeal to our human pride. It may pander to our self-centered preoccupation with self-improvement. But it is not the teaching of God's Word. Nor is it endorsed by our Lord.

Throughout the Scriptures, the Spirit of God reiterates again and again that our human nature is not righteous—that we are not normally good people who can at will, if we so choose, produce good fruit.

The picture presented to us in unmistakable language is that there must be the divine life of the living God implanted in our spirits. The very seed of the life of Christ sown in us by the Spirit of God can germinate in the ground of our being to mature into magnificent fruitage if we permit it to happen.

"It is the spirit that quickeneth; the flesh (my human nature) profiteth nothing: the words that I speak unto you, they are spirit and they are life" (John 6:63).

As this good seed from the Spirit of God germinates in the garden of my life it will begin to flourish and mature. Ripened fruit will eventually emerge. In some lives this will produce fruit thirty, sixty, and even a hundred times the amount originally planted.

Love Lies at the Root

That amazing love of God will have been reproduced supernaturally, through divine diligence, in a human being. God Himself looks upon the toil and travail of His own soul and is satisfied. He has gotten Himself a crop. The worldling looks on and must admit to himself: "This one is a child of God! He is different—distinctly and decisively."

It must be emphasized here that I have the love of God only to the extent that I have God Himself.

God does not dispense the fruits of His Spirit apart from Himself!

To put it another way: I only have the love of God to the degree that God lives His life in and through me. God does not drop neat, glittering, gift-wrapped packages of His sweet fruit into my life. We may pray for that to happen, and we may think it can. It never does. We are deluded if we think it will. When we ask God to give us the precious fruits of His own Spirit, these are bestowed always and only through the increased presence of His own person.

The more I have Christ the more I have His love.

The more I have God the more I have His goodness.

The more I have the Holy Spirit the more I have His wholeness.

And this total righteousness, wholesomeness, gracious goodness of the life of God finds full expression to one degree or another in all the nine facets of fruitfulness listed by the apostle Paul in Galatians 5:22 and 23.

Let me illustrate to point out exactly and clearly what is implied by the foregoing.

A head of wheat, barley or oats may contain in itself nine individual, separate, and distinct kernels of grain. Each kernel differs from the others in its own particular shape, size, and content. Yet all nine kernels are from the same source. They are all either wheat, oats, or barley depending upon the plant that produced them. One may be full and round and plump, another may be somewhat shrunken or shriveled. Still they are all either oats or wheat or barley because they were collectively borne upon the same stalk and came from the same seed.

A similar illustration can be given from a cluster of grapes. If the cluster contains nine individual fruits, they will each be the same sort of fruit, though they may differ slightly in size, shape, and taste. One grape in the cluster may be fully ripened, full of sweet juice, pleasing to the eye and delectable to taste. But in the same cluster there may also be several grapes which are somewhat less ripe, rather green, still sour or perhaps even shrunken and shriveled. Still they are all the same grapes growing on a single stem from the same vine.

So it is with the life of God, the love of God that we may say grows from the single stalk of the life of the Spirit of God in us. The individual grape of *joy* may be very fully matured in my life, but at the same time that of *patience* may be decidedly small, sour, and shrunken.

With this thought then in the background of our understanding we can look at the love of God and see it in practical terms that remove it from the realm of theory, theology, or ivory tower teaching. We will see this life of God portrayed for us in practical, everyday realities that produce fruits of wholesome (holy), right (righteous) living.

Love Is Selflessness

To begin with it is imperative to paint out here that the "love of God" referred to so freely, especially in the New Testament, is *selflessness:*

It is *self-giving.*
It is *self-sharing.*
It is *self-sacrificing.*
It is *self-losing.*
It is *self-abandonment.*
It is *self-serving others.*

This kind of love found its supreme and most sublime expression in the life and death of our Lord Jesus Christ. He was the visible expression to our humanity of the Invisible God. He was the love of God demonstrated indelibly in the perfect doing and perfect dying of deity. His transcendent life revealed the true nature of God. There simply was no greater means by which He could manifest His own character.

The love of God was shown to be one with the life of God. In no way could the one be separated from the other. They are one and the same.

This is why the apostle John without apology or hesitation declared flatly: ". . . *God Is Love*" (1 John 4:8).

This caliber and kind of love is not to be confused with erotic love. Nor is it to be equated with filial love. Both of the latter also have their origin with God. It was He who initiated them as part and parcel of the magnificent interrelationships which can make family life so thrilling and satisfying.

But the love of God, so-called *agape* love in the Greek, is essentially selflessness finding form in nine distinct facets. For purposes of simplicity and clarity here are those nine fruits all taken from the same cluster, or those nine kernels all drawn from the same head:

GALATIANS 5:22, 23	1 CORINTHIANS 13:1–7
1. *Love*	Does not seek her own, is not selfish or self-centered.
2. *Joy*	Love does not rejoice in iniquity but rather rejoices in the truth.
3. *Peace*	Love is not easily provoked, but is serene and stable.
4. *Longsuffering*	Love suffers long, perseveres, is patient.
5. *Kindness (gentleness)*	Love is merciful, thoughtful, and concerned; it envies not.
6. *Goodness*	Love is great, gracious, and generous; it is kind and good.
7. *Faithfulness*	Love thinks no evil but has faith in God and others.
8. *Meekness*	Love is humble and gentle, does not vaunt itself.
9. *Temperance*	Love is disciplined and controlled, does not behave unbecomingly.

Even a cursory glance at the content of God's love discloses that here we are face to face with a powerful, potent life principle. We are dealing with a divine dimension of living, a radical life style.

God grant that within us there might be generated an enormous, overwhelming, irresistible desire to become like Him who is *love* . . . to have reproduced in us the fruit of His life.

Love Is the Very Life of God

If we pause momentarily to reflect on the practical out-working of such love in our everyday world it may well be the first seed with a spiritual germ to be dropped into the soil of our souls. Here I quote, without apology, from my book *Rabboni.*

"In all the enterprises which engaged this tremendous triumvirate, there are perfect coordination of concept and ultimate unity of purpose in their planning. Unlike human endeavors, it was never marked by discord. Friction was unknown simply because there was no selfish self-interest present. Between God the Father, God the Son Jesus Christ, and God the Holy Spirit there flowed love in its most sublime form. In fact, this love was of such purity that it constituted the very basis of their beings. It was the essence of their characters.

"We earthmen can barely conceive of a relationship so sublime that it contains no trace of self-assertion, no ulterior motive nor self-gratification. But that is the secret to the strength of God. Here was demonstrated the irresistible force of utter selflessness. In the total giving of each to the other, in profound CARING for each other, lay the love of all eternity. This was love at its loftiest level. This was love at its highest source. This was love, the primal source of all energy.

"Just as there is stored within an atom enormous power because of the interaction between neutrons, protons, and electrons, likewise there was inherent unlimited energy in the Godhead because of the interrelationship between Father, Son, and Spirit. And the essence of this energy was love.

"In that outer world love was the moving force behind every action. Love was the energizing influence at work in every enterprise. Love was the very fiber woven into every aspect of Christ's life. It was in fact the basic raw material used ultimately to fashion and form all subsequent matter.

"To the reader this may all seem a bit obscure, a bit beyond belief. But if we pause to find parallels upon our planet, earth, we may soon see the picture in practical terms. What is the most irresistible force upon the earth? Love! What pulverizes strong prejudice and builds enduring allegiance? Love! What binds men together in indestructible devotion? Love!

"What underlies all generous and magnanimous actions? Love! What is the source of strength for men and women who gladly serve and die for one another? Love! What energizes the loftiest and most noble enterprise of human hearts and minds? Love! If this be true of selfish mortal men, then how much more is it the very life of God—and this is the life of Christ."

Obviously such love is not insipid and sentimental. It is strong as steel; tough as tungsten; enduring as a diamond. It is the essence of the eternal.

This love of God is nothing less than the life of God poured out lavishly and constantly. It is what

THE NINE FACETS OF GOD'S LOVE

energizes the cosmos. And only when we are brought into full harmony with its own on-going purposes can we sense and know that at last we too are caught up in the grand will of God. Only then do we discover the delight of moving strongly and surely in the supreme designs of God. Then the most minute details of life bear enormous meaning and purpose.

My Own Experience

You may well wonder how to reach a point where you too can come to receive this love—how you can open your life to allow this new divine quickening of a higher life to enter the soil of your own soul. Perhaps my own experience will help someone to understand a little better.

As my fortieth year of life drew to a close, there crept over my spirit an acute awareness that there was something significant lacking. It was not in the realm of material or moral values. I had a beautiful wife whom I loved deeply. I had wholesome, alert, fine children. The business endeavors in which my strength and energy had been invested were remarkably successful. I had gained financial independence and security. Every aim and ambition set for myself as a young man had been achieved and even surpassed.

But in spite of such apparent success, deep within my spirit was the inescapable conviction that I was missing the mark. The main purpose for which I had been placed upon the planet was being bypassed. I simply was not moving strongly with the stream of God's best intentions for me.

There then began a desperate search to discover what the dilemma was. Where was the difficulty? Perhaps because of my very formidable self-will, my determined drives, or even the slowness of my stony soul I could not seem to see that I had lived pretty much for selfish, self-centered purposes. They had dominated my days.

The malaise of my life came from a lack of love—God's love—a lack of selflessness and self-giving to Him and to others. But once I saw this great, spiritual vacuum within, virtually void of the life of God—the love of Christ—an insatiable, overwhelming, all-consuming desire was generated to have His Spirit sweep into my soul. He alone could satisfy that fierce yearning for fruitfulness and productivity.

The crisis came one mellow autumn day in the foothills of the Rockies. Alone, in anguish of spirit I went to hike along the high cliffs bordering a deep coulee. Down in its depths ran a crystal clear stream of ice-cold water. It flowed from the glaciers and ice fields of the snow-mantled mountains shining in the west.

"O God," I cried out from the depths of my being, "come flooding into my spirit; into my soul; into my entire body and being. O Christ, come in like these snow-fed waters from the high country stream down into this valley. O Spirit of the Living God, pour into this parched and barren soil of mine. Shed abroad in me the very life of God—the love of Christ.

Fit me to be good ground in which the seed of your good Word can take root and flourish and prosper."

It was a heart cry of utter desperation. For five full hours I tramped up and down that lonely canyon trail in awesome anguish of soul. If ever a man hungered and thirsted after righteousness—the right life of God—I did that day.

The gentle, gracious, yet galvanizing response of God's Gracious Spirit to my cries came as a surprise: "If you will just comply with *My* wishes; carry out *My* commands; cooperate with *My* desires I will give Myself to you in abundant measure. *I give Myself—My life—My love—My Spirit* wholeheartedly to those who obey *Me.*"

It meant my priorities in life suddenly had to be reversed. Life was no longer to be lived for *myself,* but for *Him* and *His.* It was the beginning of a brand new relationship with God. As I complied with His wishes in everyday details, His life and His love flooded in to produce eternal, enduring fruit.

Looking back over the intervening years I marvel at the generosity of God. He took a barren life and in His own gracious way made it bountiful.

He will do it for anyone who will seriously and sincerely open themselves, becoming available to His Presence.

SIX

Joy in the Christian's Life

In the grand and deeply moving prophecy of the ancient prophet Isaiah, it was foretold that when Christ came He would impart to His people *"the oil of joy"* for mourning (Isa. 61:3). Joy has ever been one of the most significant hallmarks of God's people. It is a unique quality of character often confused with happiness.

Joy and happiness are not the same.

Each springs from a totally different source.

One comes from the world around me. The other originates directly with the Spirit of the Living God.

Happiness is conditioned by and often dependent upon what is "happening" to me. It is irrevocably bound up either with the behavior of other people, the sequence of events in my life, or the circumstances in which I find myself.

If these are going well in one way or another I am said to be "happy." If, on the other hand, my circumstances are adverse I am described as "unhappy."

For the most part "happy" or "happiness" are words that belong very much to the world. They are seldom used in Scripture (about six times in the New Testament, perhaps sixteen in the Old). And when they are employed it is generally in the traditional Anglo-Saxon meaning of being well-favored or very fortunate. An example is Psalm 144:15b ". . . *Happy* (fortunate—well-favored) is that people, whose God is the Lord."

The Nature of True Joy

Joy, on the other hand, appears in a variety of forms such as "joyful" or "rejoice" (about eight times more often than does happiness). It throbs throughout the Scriptures as a profound, compelling quality of life that surmounts and transcends the events and disasters which may dog God's people. Joy is a divine dimension of living not shackled by circumstances.

This joy springs from the presence of God in a person's life. It is frequently referred to as "the joy of the Lord," or "joy in the Holy Spirit." It is in no way dependent either upon people around me, the course of events in my experience, or the circumstances in which I find myself, be they ever so calamitous or fortunate.

Joy is one of the grand attributes of God Himself.

It is an integral part of His character. Joy runs like a sparkling stream of great good-will through His makeup. Known as the God of all joy, He rejoices in all His own accomplishments. He is joyful in His own delectable character.

When we discover for ourselves that God our Father really is like this it endears Him to us in a delightful way. He is not an august, austere, awesome judge standing aloof and apart from us in the agony of our human anguish. He is the one who yearns over us, longs for us, searches for us, and when we are found enfolds us to Himself with inexpressible joy.

He is the Good Gardener who toils over us and tends us with constant care. Patiently he waits for the full fruitage. He finds joy in the planting He has done, and He waits eagerly for a crop. With great joy He gathers the harvest.

There is deep delight in all He does.

There is enthusiasm in everything He undertakes.

There is sweet satisfaction in all His enterprises.

His life, vitality, enthusiasm, and energy are transmitted directly to me by His Spirit who resides within.

It is His knowledge of me, His careful husbanding of the ground of my being, His concern for my welfare, His cultivation of my character, His constant presence in the garden of my little life—that guarantees my joy. For little by little I come to discover that He is totally trustworthy. I learn that no matter how unpredictable people may prove, or how exasperating events may be, or how crushing circumstances may seem, He is still there (here), utterly reliable.

Because of His total integrity and absolute honesty and constant love expressed to me as His person I am charged with joy.

The Joy-Love Connection

This is what Paul means in writing about love in 1 Corinthians 13. He declares without hesitation,

"Love rejoices in the truth."

It is the love of God, the life of God grounded and founded upon His own infallible character. He simply cannot betray either Himself or those in His care. He is bound to bring the best out of any life under His care. It simply cannot be otherwise. And therein lies our joy.

He does all things well.

He is able to do abundantly more than we can ask or even imagine.

He can bring good out of what to us seems evil.

He can take our desolate wilderness lives and turn them into a glorious garden.

He finds joy in such a labor of love.

And it is in the process of pouring His very own life into us that there springs up from the stony, weedy, hard-packed pathway soil of my soul joy: The joy of *knowing He is at work in me and I am under His care.*

Slowly but surely the seed of His good Word germinates in the ground of my life. There emerges from the bareness of my soul a new life with new values, new standards, new concepts based upon *truth,* upon the *verities* of God in Christ.

What before may have seemed folly and foolishness to my worldly-wise mind suddenly begins to make sense. Spiritual insights imparted and implanted in my spirit by God's Gracious Spirit take root and mature. Joy, enormous joy in God, in having found truth, in discovering the true dimension of deeply satisfying life sweeps into my spirit expelling the skepticism and cynicism of my former life.

Perhaps this is the point to pause and explain why people do become such skeptics apart from God. Some of us don't really understand why, in spite of humanity's desperate quest for happiness, most men and women still lack genuine joy. A person may have succeeded in every area of life and still feel he/she has missed the mark. Such a person hasn't found joy . . . that enduring quality that far transcends transient happiness.

Joy vs. Happiness

Happiness is extremely vulnerable. It is insecure and unsure. At best it is established on unreliable, unpredictable ground.

Happiness wrapped up in people can be torn and tortured. Even our dearest family members, friends or business associates can play us false. Sometimes those who once were fond of each other come to hate and despise one another. Trust turns to distrust.

Happiness centered in wealth or possessions or property is extremely hazardous. Everything (except God) is subject to change and the fluctuations of fad and fashion. The inexorable forces of decay, deterioration, devaluation, and depreciation are everywhere at work in the world. A person expends his time, strength, and thought to amass possessions only to see them fade before his eyes.

Often instead of owning what they have labored to accumulate, they discover that they in turn are "owned" by their possessions. Such people have become enslaved. They are worn and weary wondering if they will lose what they have won.

Happiness based merely on buoyant good health is a delusion. Time takes its toll even amongst the most handsome of men and beautiful of women. Vigor wanes; beauty fades; reflexes slow down; eyes grow dim; hearing fails; teeth fall out; memory falters; and body vitality diminishes.

Happiness grounded in a successful career or outstanding social achievement is invariably short-lived. Soon another new star rises on the horizon to eclipse one's finest accomplishments. Records are broken and fall every year. Names and faces once famous are quickly forgotten to fade into the mists of oblivion.

So the list could go on. The sum total of human enterprise and initiative is like mist that disappears with the sun. It comes eventually to a mere shadow—a mocking memory. The owner is left with lingering skepticism and bitter disillusionment. Subconsciously he feels cheated and double-crossed.

In vain the worldling turns desperately and despairingly to drink from any broken cistern or muddied water that he thinks might slake his thirst for joy. But all disappoints him. For only in God Himself can the source of joy be found.

Surprised by Joy

In brilliant, blazing contrast the person who permits God in Christ, by His Spirit, to come sweeping into his spirit, is overwhelmingly surprised by joy. The sweet, gracious, generous Spirit of the Lord enlivens him. The very mainspring of life is touched. The quickening influence of the Divine Presence permeates the entire person. A diametrically new, dynamic dimension of living pervades the life so that the whole of the soul (mind, emotions, will) as well as the body (physical makeup) come alive to the Gracious Spirit of the risen Christ now resident within.

This is to know the government of God in my life, to actually experience the control of Christ in my conduct and conversation. It is to sense the sovereignty of the Spirit of God bringing order out of confusion, direction out of despair, and joy out of despondency.

Millions of men and women across the centuries attest to this transformation in their lives. It is what is meant by Paul in Romans 14:17, "The kingdom of God is not meat and drink: but righteousness and peace and *joy in the Holy Ghost*" (italics mine). God is here! He is alive! He is in charge!

This was the irresistible dynamic of the early church. It is still the experience of anyone who truly allows God to enter the garden of his/her life. Enthusiasm and deep delight pervades such a person. There is direction in his/her endeavors no matter how mundane or menial. There is purpose and profound meaning to the minutiae of life. A piece of common clay of ordinary humanity has come under the hand of the Divine Husbandman. And the fruit of joy springs from the soil of that soul.

This joy is not that of selfish self-interest in who I am. Rather it is the joy of *knowing God* at last and realizing that *He knows me.* It lies in the serene surprise of how generous and joyful is His presence.

The Joy of Forgiveness

Combined with this comes the sweet consolation and exquisite joy of knowing that because of His gracious redemption my sins are forgiven, the guilt is gone, and I am accepted into His family.

In a profoundly purifying way His Spirit sweeps through my being to assure me that I am right with God and He with me. I am made right with others and they are made right with me. A deep, settled assurance that all is well even between me and myself descends upon my spirit. This is to have and know the joy of the Lord. It becomes a formidable force in the very fabric of my life. It is literally a great light illuminating the whole of my interior, dispelling the darkness and despair that formerly dominated my deepest desires.

All of this is so because *He is here.*
Christ has come.
His Spirit is in residence.
God is in the garden on my life.

Counterfeit Joy

Out of a sense of solemn responsibility to the reader I must state here that there is such a thing as counterfeit joy. It is one of the calamities of Christendom that often people will pursue pleasant sensations believing implicitly that the gratification of sensual desire is to know the joy of the Lord. This is a dreadful delusion that frequently leads the victim to even deeper despair and dismay.

It is perfectly possible to produce the illusion of joy in crowds by the use of emotional mood music, "soul" songs, so called; syncopated rhythms; a swinging "beat"; all can generate deep emotional responses assumed to be joy.

The same is true of sensationalism in preaching—the use of sentimental stories or overdramatization of a person's delivery. Reliance is placed upon sensuality rather than upon the Spirit of God to convict, enlighten, and convert the soul.

Likewise in "sharing" sessions where undue emphasis is placed upon physical contact between persons—where people are encouraged to indulge in hugging, kissing, laughing or crying together there lurks the danger of being deceived by counterfeit joy.

What the victim is experiencing is happiness, either from the music, the manipulated message, or the mood of his associates. Relying upon the people or events around him, He is not experiencing the joy of God's gentle Spirit at work in his spirit.

Counterfeit joy is a passing, titillating, unpredictable sensation that temporarily transcends the despondency of the moment. To seek it is to drink from a sensual source that ever leaves the thirsting, questing spirit unsatisfied, often disillusioned and in subsequent despair.

To know the true joy of the Lord, present always in profound, quiet, still, inner power, because of His presence within, is to have the capacity to triumphantly transcend all the turmoil of our times in strength.

The Source of Joy

It may be asked, how does one get this strong joy? It comes only with Him who Himself is the God of all joy. The extent to which He occupies the ground of my whole being, that is the extent to which I have His joy.

If Christ controls and has His way in my career, business, hobbies, home, friendships, service, and interests, whatever they be, there I will also experience His joy.

It is quite literally impossible to be at variance with God in any area of life and there find joy. Joy is part and parcel of harmony with Him in my activities. The instant I comply with His wishes, His joy energizes my being. The moment I disagree with His desires joy fades, and faith falters.

As Christ comes into our affairs His desire is that our attention and interest be refocused on Him. It is He who is at work within us both to will and do of His own good pleasure (Phil 2:13). Too often we are preoccupied with the process of fruit production rather than the Good Gardener who is responsible for the fruitage. Too often we are looking for joy when we should just be looking away to Jesus Christ. Our joy is in Him. Our strength is in His ability to produce the joy.

As He moves over the ground of my life, cultivating, tending, loving every corner of it, He will be at work asking me to respond. If in simple obedience I will comply by giving myself away, losing myself for others, there will spring to life the joy of His Spirit in my spirit.

"It is God, not we, who made the garden grow in your hearts" (1 Cor. 3:6, LB).

SEVEN

Peace and Peacemakers

In the world around, amongst all men, Christian and non-Christian, peace is regarded as one of the supreme attainments. In the tumultuous history of the twentieth century perhaps no other single subject has occupied more prominence in the hopes, dreams, and aspirations of mankind. Peace is ever upon peoples' minds and lips. It is the profound longing of uncounted millions. Peace is the prize sought for in the depths of the human soul, yet the attribute so often absent.

Why? Why is it so ardently desired yet so seldom discovered?

Why are the Scriptures so true when they declare that men shall cry: "Peace, peace, when there is no peace!" (Jer. 6:14; 8:11).

Why do so few ever find the path to peace?

The Nature of Peace

The answer lies largely in our basic human misunderstanding of what peace is and how it is produced.

Our Lord, while living here amongst us, placed such a remarkable priority upon peace that He made the amazing statement: "Blessed are the peacemakers (i.e. those who produce peace): for they shall be called the children of God" (Matt. 5:9).

It is appropriate, therefore, to discover what peace really is. As long as we labor under a delusion as to its true character and identity it will ever elude us.

First of all, peace is not just passivity. It is not merely stagnation. It is not sterility. It is not a negative attitude of non-involvement.

The production of peace calls for powerful and a most pronounced action on the part of the peacemaker. The path of peace which God's Word instructs us to pursue is not strewn softly with rose petals. Rather it is a tough trail tramped out with humble heart and lowly spirit despite its rough rocks of adversity.

Peace is the selfless, self-giving, self-losing, self-forgetting, self-sacrificing love of God in repose despite all the adverse reverses of life. It is love standing serene, strong, and stable in spite of every insult, every antagonism, every hate.

Peace is the spirit and soul of persons so imbued with the presence of God's Gracious Spirit that they are not easily provoked: They are not "touchy." They are not irritable or easily enraged. Their pride is not readily pricked. They do not live like a bristling porcupine with all its quills extended in agitated self-defense.

Peace is actually the exact opposite. It is the quiet, potent, gracious attitude of serenity and good-will that comes to meet the onslaught of others with good cheer, equanimity, and strong repose.

To see and understand this quality of life at its best we simply must turn away from our contemporaries and look at Christ . . . God very God.

The God of All Peace

He is known as the God of all peace. He alone is the source and supplier of peace. Active in our attitudes and actions, he alone can produce this quality of life in our everyday experiences.

All through human history God has approached men in peace. Always He has come amongst us with good-will. This was dramatized in the incredible declaration of the angels on the night of His advent: "On earth, peace good will toward men" (Luke 2:14)!

This has ever been God's generous, magnanimous approach to humanity, despite man's most despicable hatred and opposition to His overtures of good will. It matters not where God's Spirit finds a man or woman, His approach is always in peace. It matters not how deep the sin, how dark the stain, how set the soul in selfishness—Christ comes to us in peace.

He has our redemption in view and our ultimate renewal in mind. He has our restoration to His family as the supreme goal of His own goodness. He comes to us with arms outstretched, with brimming eyes that have looked upon us with longing, with His Spirit spilling over with good will.

> Behold, I will bring it health and cure, and I will cure them, and will reveal unto them the abundance of peace and truth.
>
> And I will cause the captivity of Judah and the captivity of Israel to return, and will build them, as at the first.
>
> And I will cleanse them from all their iniquity, whereby they have sinned against me; and I will pardon all their iniquities, whereby they have sinned, and whereby they have transgressed against me.
>
> And it shall be to me a name of joy, a praise and an honour before all the nations of the earth, which shall hear all the good that I do unto them: and they shall fear and tremble for all the prosperity and for all the goodness that I procure unto it (Jer. 33:6–9).

This is the true nature and character of God revealed in His dealing with difficult and disagreeable people.

Jesus, the Man of Peace

Even when here amongst us as a man He came in peace. It was the impact of this peace that touched and transformed people as tough as tax collectors, prostitutes, and cursing fishermen. It was the incredible impact of this peace that turned James and John, the flaming, flashing "sons of thunder," into beloved apostles of love. It was the impulse of this peace, this love in action, that made Christ cry out in the midst of His own crushing agony, "Father, forgive them, for they know not what they do!" (Luke 23:34).

He was at peace with His enemies.

They were at war with Him.

He Himself, to explain this enigma, had stated clearly on one occasion: "I came not to send peace, but a sword" (Matt. 10:34). For in His very coming people were polarized. Those whose spirits responded positively to the overtures of His divine love and peace would be passionately fond of Him. Those repelled by His truth and integrity would hate with appalling venom, determined to destroy Him.

It is ever thus. God does not change. Christ does not alter His approach to men. The Gracious Spirit comes always in peace to convict, correct, and convert men. The human response to that coming determines whether in fact men enjoy peace or remain engulfed in terrible hostility.

The Source of Peace

If the life is opened to receive the divine presence of the risen Christ, He comes in, speaking peace— just as He came again and again to His distraught disciples after His resurrection, saying, *"Peace be unto you!"*

He comes into our lives there to shed abroad a new love, His own life, that expresses itself in peace. When He enters my experience; when He penetrates my personality; when He becomes Sovereign in my spirit, I in turn become a person of peace. It is then that I begin to know what it means to be at peace with God, at peace with others, at peace with myself.

Increasingly as He is given control of my life the entire complexion of my character, conduct, and conversation alters. I discover that He can change me dramatically. Peace, good will, good cheer, and serenity replace animosity, bitterness, hostility, belligerence, jealousy, bad temper, quarreling, and rivalry.

In passing it should be pointed out that these latter attitudes are those listed specifically in Galatians 5:19, 20 as being indicators of the old, unchanged life. People who express such emotions and give vent to such feelings and attitudes are not "peacemakers"—rather they are "problem producers."

Such people produce enormous pain for both themselves and others. They alienate friends, family, and associates, building formidable barriers of ill will between themselves and others. They injure, wound, and grieve those around them. Often their dearest friends and family suffer most because of the despair, darkness, and dismay generated by their anger.

This anger aroused, inflamed, and vented upon others is the exact opposite of peace. Instead of being selfless love it is self-centeredness, self-preoccupation inflamed and aroused in self-defense and self-assertion.

Peace Produces Healing

On the other hand, the peace of God, which is self-sacrificing and self-foregoing, produces healing.

It comes to bind up the wounds; to pour in the oil of consolation; to bring repose and quietness; to still the troubled soul; to speak peace to stormy spirits. This peace comes only from Christ. It is one of the genuine, indisputable marks of God's presence in a person's life.

By the same measure it may be said with equal force that if peace is absent from a person's life it is apparent that Christ really has not come in. It is a delusion to believe or think one is a Christian whose life is marked by constant battling, bitterness or belligerence.

Paul put it forcefully when he stated that "They which do such things *shall not inherit the kingdom of God*" (Gal. 5:21, italics mine).

This should, of course, be obvious to anyone who thinks seriously about the subject. "For the kingdom of God is not meat and drink but righteousness and peace and joy in the Holy Ghost" (Rom. 14:17).

Lest the reader be confused it is important to point out here that the in-coming of Christ does not mean I shall have no enemies in life. It does not mean I am ushered into a utopia where all is at peace, where life becomes a gentle millpond of perfection. We simply are not given any such guarantee anywhere in God's Word. On the contrary, we are advised solemnly that God's people must be prepared to endure afflictions, to face hostility from others, to undergo tribulation, and to be hated by an adverse world.

For years, as a young man, I labored under the false assumption that if I was just gracious enough and good enough everyone would love me. In part this delusion came from false teaching. The unvarnished truth is that even God, the God of all peace, when He came to live amongst us as the perfect person was despised and rejected of men. He stated emphatically to His little band of would be followers just before His death, "If the world hate you, ye know that it hated me before it hated you" (John 15:18).

Where then, it may be asked, does peace come into the picture here? It is a legitimate question that deserves an honest answer.

That answer is best summed up in the statement made by Solomon in Proverbs 16:7, "When a man's ways please the Lord, he maketh even his enemies to be at peace with him."

It Takes Two to Quarrel

There is no guarantee that I shall not have enemies. I will. They are those polarized by the powerful presence of the Gracious Spirit of God in my life. But even they, like the tough Roman centurion who was charged with crucifying Christ, will admit, "Truly this was (a peacemaker) the Son of God" (Matt. 27:54).

The point we must see here is very important. It takes two to quarrel. If one of the two exudes good will, comes with good cheer, gives of himself in selfless love, that one is at peace. The other may still despise, hate, and abuse the first, but he remains the one with the problem, the one with the inner darkness and despair.

As God's people of peace we need not be victimized by our detractors. We can be at peace with them, as Christ was, even if they are at odds with us.

God calls us to be "big" people, strong people, serene people, steady, solid people of His caliber. We are not to be dragged down into the ditch of destructive hatreds, animosities, and mudslinging.

There is a quaint but powerful old proverb, "He who throws dirt only loses ground!" And how true that is in the garden of our lives. There are bound to be some storms of stress and strain that break around me but if the good crop of God's peaceful nature is growing luxuriantly in the ground of my being the soil of my soul will not be eroded or blown away in the downpour of hatred or winds of adversity that beat upon me.

Steps to Peace

Perhaps the most helpful thing one can do here is to explain, in very simple terms, exactly how the peace of God can become one of the most notable products of my life. There are three important steps to be taken.

1) There must be a willingness to face myself squarely. If I am an individual who fights, quarrels, finds fault, and produces problems for both myself and others, it must be admitted. In fact I must come to the solemn and very sobering conclusion that ha-

tred, belligerence, and animosity spring directly from my selfish, self-centered old nature.

This is not a question of indulging in morbid introspection. It is a matter of getting serious with God and myself about my behavior. I must come to hate my hatred!

It is utterly pointless to put up a smoke screen of childish excuses such as: "I can't help it, I'm born with a bad temper," or "I'm just an honest person and say what I think, let the chips fall where they may," or "It's all their fault, they are wrong, they give me good reason to be mad." And a hundred others like them. This is not the path to peace but of terrible peril.

Instead let me cry out in absolute earnestness, "O God, in Christ change me. Come in by Your Gracious Spirit. Let the sweet seed of Your good Word be implanted in the stony ground of my hatred-hardened heart. Let there spring up in my soul, my mind, my emotions, my will the ability to love as You love, to give myself in peace to others as You give Yourself to me."

2) If this prayer is uttered in absolute sincerity some startling things will take place. God in turn will take me seriously. He will waste no time getting to the point of dealing with my dreadful, selfish, self-centered pride. This is the root cause of hatred, ill will, and jealous animosity.

The weeds of self-assertion, self-agrandizement, self-serving, self-importance, self-assurance must go. All the old worldly concepts of personal grandeur and greatness which so readily invade our thinking will have to be plowed under by the deep in-working of the Good Gardener. It is not a painless process. It is devastating to my inflated ego and bloated self-image.

This personal pride can find expression in a hundred ways, most of them apparently legitimate. Wherever I am proud, that is where I am also provocatively touchy. Wherever I congratulate myself, there I am terribly sensitive to hurt. So God will have to cut down these competing weeds. He has remarkable ways of humbling me in a hurry. He can allow the blight of events to touch my health, my home, my family, my friends, my career, my finances, my achievements, and bring them all down to dust.

But it is the humbled person, the lowly person, who finally finds rest and repose. He is no longer on a pedestal from which he can be knocked to the ground. He has come to practical terms and a realistic relationship with God, with others, with himself.

3) As this process goes on in our lives there is often a tendency for us to ask God to relent. There comes a time when we are tempted to ask Him to stop the plowing, to stop clearing the land, to quit the deep cultivation of our characters. Let us not do so. It is for our good and for fruit.

Peace comes as pride goes.

Peace will replace arrogance.

Peace will grow where animosity formerly flourished.

The person of humbled heart and contrite spirit in the care of a loving Husbandman is a person of peace. Our lives can be like a well-watered garden of Eden. They need not be bloody battlegrounds of bitterness. The world without may be at war all around us. But within, His presence, His life, His Spirit produces peace making me a peacemaker.

EIGHT

Patience

The word "patience" as it is used in the New Testament, really has no true equivalent in the English language. Certainly it does not mean merely being placid and phlegmatic as so many people assume.

Patience is the powerful capacity of selfless love to suffer long under adversity. It is that noble ability to bear with either difficult people or adverse circumstances without breaking down. This implies that one has a certain degree of tolerance for the intolerable. It is a generous willingness to try to understand the awkward people or disturbing events that our Father allows to enter our lives.

Over and beyond all of these, patience is that powerful attribute that enables a man or woman to remain steadfast under strain, not just standing still but pressing on. Patience is the potent perseverance that produces positive results even under opposition and suffering. It is love, gracious, self-giving, pressing on, enduring hardship, because of the benefit it may bring to others. It is a quiet willingness to wait, alert and watchful for the right moment to make the appropriate move.

What Patience Is Not

Patience is not being phlegmatic or lethargic. It is not indolence or indifference. It is not that fatalistic attitude toward life which sits back, twiddles its thumbs, and hums: "Whatever will be, will be. . . ."

There is nothing weak, insipid or flaccid about it. It is a force of enormous power and influence— that one of God's attributes which, when exhibited in the life of His person, startles and astounds us.

So often we human beings, rather than exercising patience, prefer to opt out of adversity. Endeavoring to escape from difficult situations, we try to avoid and cut ourselves off from awkward people. We kick over the traces, shake off the harness, and break up anything that might bind us into suffering.

Yet the patience of God spoken of in the New Testament is just the opposite. It is really a picture of a beast of burden remaining steadily under control. It is an ox yoked to a plow breaking up the stiff soil of its owner's field. No matter whether the plow runs into rocks, stumps or heavy sod, the patient beast just pushes on steadily. Regardless of summer sun, the annoyance of flies or chilling winds the strong beast goes on breaking ground for its master.

The patience of the New Testament writers is that of a small donkey bearing enormous burdens of firewood, sacks of grain or other produce for its owner. Year in, year out, surely, steadily, safely it transports loads of goods from place to place in quiet compliance with its master's wishes.

This patience is a camel or colt or bullock harnessed to a circular treadmill. There hour after hour, day upon day it moves steadily lifting water to irrigate some little parched plot of ground. Or it may be thrashing out wheat to feed a hungry village. It is all part and parcel of achieving worthy ends through suffering service.

Christ—A Picture of Patience

This quality of character was beautifully displayed for us in the life of our Lord. He, the Christ, came amongst us as the Suffering Servant. He came, not to be ministered to, but to minister (serve). And the gracious perseverance with which He endured every adversity as well as the abuse of evil men for our sakes and our salvation stirs our souls.

Were it not for the longsuffering patience of our God in dealing with us difficult human beings, where would we be? Long ago the human race would have perished because of perverseness, pride, and the pollution of our characters. But for the patient longsuffering of a Gracious God men could not for a moment stand in His impeccable and wholly righteous presence.

Only as we come to see and appreciate this fact will we bow humbly before Him and beg His pardon.

It is only the patient willingness of a generous Father to put up with us, to understand us, and to persevere with us that gives us great hope and good cheer.

Looking back over my own life I tremble to think where I would be but for the loving patience of the Lord in dealing with me. How unrelentingly His Gracious Spirit pursued me down the tangled, twisted trails of my own selfish choosing. How He put up with my pride and perverseness as a self-assured person.

Just reflecting quietly upon this incredible attribute of Christ's loving concern for me crumbles my pride and stills me before Him.

This is the love of God in action—the quiet, strong, persevering determination of divinity to do me nothing but great good. For years and years God's Gracious Spirit came seeking and searching for my soul in good will. Despite my stubbornness, folly, waywardness and confusion He never relented. He never grew weary.

Ultimately it was His patience which prevailed. His perseverance pulverized my resistance. It dawned one day upon my dull and sin-stained spirit that He really cared, and cared deeply for this empty shell of a man, whose life He longed to fill and revive with His own abundant life.

It is this quality in the character of God to which I here refer. And it is an attribute of His own enormous love which He eagerly wants to share with His people. In fact, this is one of the fruits of His own Gracious Spirit which He endeavors to cultivate with care in our lives, if we will allow Him to do so. He comes to the garden of His own looking for it. Sometimes it can scarcely be found.

This is doubly strange when one stops to consider how patient He has been with us. Jesus told a story to illustrate this point. It is related in Matthew 18:21–33. One man who had an enormous debt asked his creditor to be patient with him until he paid. Yet he in turn went out and demanded immediate settlement from one who owed him a mere pittance.

Many of us are like that. This is not the love of God.

We tend to chop people down. By nature we are demanding and harsh. We want our pound of flesh from the next person; we will not put up with poor performance on the part of others. We want almost instant results, and we will not give others the benefit of the doubt or wait to see what God can do in their lives. We will not prevail in prayer for them.

In the case of adversity or difficult circumstances we want "out." Looking for the nearest exit, we duck and dodge to free ourselves from any unpleasant situation. We even pray earnestly to be delivered from every difficult or demanding experience.

All of this is the opposite of love in action. Love means I will push on in spite of obstacles. Love means being willing to suffer and endure the slings and stones of life. And love perseveres against formidable odds, just simply "keeping on."

When even a small glimmer of this grace takes root in our lives by the in-working of God's own Spirit some astonishing things happen, both to us and others.

The Effect of Patience

Perhaps the most amazing thing is the manner in which our conduct generates hope and optimism in those around us. Even the most difficult people, drowned in despair, lost in their own selfish self-centeredness, will gain hope when they find someone who will be patient and persevere with them—who will pray for them unceasingly.

The very fact that someone cares enough to keep coming back again and again will begin to convince them that all is not wrong in the world.

Patience in God's people is one of the surest signs whereby even a non-Christian can discern and discover something of the nature of God. This attitude will pulverize the nonbeliever's prejudice more surely than almost any other Christian virtue. It will encourage him, reassure him, and convince him that there is more to Christianity than mere theory.

The Benefits of Patience

For the child of God the development of patience has two enormous benefits. First it produces within his own character tremendous strength and endurance. A better word to use is "toughness"—not tough in the sense of being rough or rowdy, but rather tough in one's ability to endure hard people and hard situations with serenity and stability.

Secondly as we are patient under adversity we discover the great faithfulness of our God to us in every situation. Little by little we learn the practical truth of that great statement made by Paul in Philippians 2:13, *"It is God who worketh in you both to will and to do of his good pleasure."*

Patience Is a Learning Experience

This fruit of God's Spirit is not something we pray for, expecting God to drop it down into our little lives like a neatly wrapped gift package. If we pray earnestly for the gift of this special grace, God will arrange for such people and circumstances to enter our experience that only the presence and exercise of His patience will enable us to cope at all. Thus we will learn to practice patience in the fierce furnace of affliction.

We will quickly find out that we do not go through life fighting the people or problems put in our path— we do not quarrel and complain with our lot in life. Nor do we try to slip out of every sticky situation. We are not those who look for just the soft spot and the comfy corner.

Instead we face whatever arrangements God our Father makes for us as His proper and appropriate provision for us. We accept these as the great, good mills of God that will grind us into fine flour to feed His hungry people. We recognize our trials as the winepress of God's own creation in which our lives can be so compressed that there will flow from us refreshment for the weary, thirsty world around us.

In such acceptance there lies peace, but also beyond that there also emerges patience. Not a grudging, shriveled sort of sour stoicism, but a cheerful delight in the divine work of the Master Gardener in my life. The deep spading and the heavy plowing of God's Spirit in my soul are what eventually will produce the rich fruit of His own patience in my character. It can come no other way.

In all of this as I continually remind myself that He, God very God, is dealing with me in patience and perseverance, I will lift up my heart and spirit to rejoice. I will rest in the sure confidence and quiet knowledge that He does all things well, both for my sake and His own.

It is when the actual awareness of Christ Himself in our lives steals over our spirits that we become still before Him. We sense that His gracious Spirit can and is conveying to our characters both the peace of God in adversity and the patience of God in tough situations.

This is to know something of Christlike contentment. We are not bent on battling and battering our way through the thickets and obstacles of life. We stand strong and sturdy, serene in the quiet assurance that "All things can and do work out for good to those who love God, who are called to be His contented people amid a very complex and conflicting culture" (Rom. 8:28, paraphrased).

It is God who empowers us to face the fever of living with good cheer and gracious optimism. For He is with us both in our joys and in our extremities. So all is well. We can be at peace and we can also be patient. This is good news for all of us.

NINE

Kindness– Love–Showing Mercy

Those readers familiar with the authorized version (King James translation) of the New Testament will wonder why kindness is here listed as the fifth fruit. I use the word kindness simply because it is employed by all the modern translations. The latter then use "gentleness" for the word "meekness" which is the eighth fruit. To avoid confusion the word kindness is used here in all of its simplicity and grandeur.

Of all the fruits of God's Gracious Spirit this is perhaps the one with which most of us are somewhat familiar. We have had this facet of love expressed to us in wondrous ways. In turn there have been times when in our own best moments we, too, have shown great kindness to others. This healing, compassionate, merciful virtue that ebbs and flows amongst us is sometimes called "the milk of human kindness."

Kindness is invariably associated with mercy. It is impossible to be kind without being merciful. Likewise to be merciful is to be kind. It implies that there is a deep and geniune concern for another. This concern is one of compassion and mercy. We are moved to be kind because we care. Caring is the essence of God's selfless love expressed to another.

Kindness is also bound up tightly with honesty and respect. It embraces the whole ideal of dealing with another person in deep integrity. Because I regard and respect others as individuals, regardless of their culture, creed, color or social standing, I treat them in a kindly manner. I endeavor to be helpful and understanding because of a genuine interest in them.

Surprisingly enough human beings are exceedingly sensitive in this area of personal relationships. They can detect in an instant if one is acting in either a patronizing or condescending way. True kindness is not tainted or tarnished with haughtiness. It is leveling with others in love, reaching out to help where it hurts.

The Cost of Kindness

This facet of love is bound to cost a great deal. Kindness is more than running a bluff on beleaguered people. It is more than pretending to be concerned by their condition. True kindness goes beyond the play acting of simulated sighs and crocodile tears. It is getting involved with the personal sorrows and strains of other lives to the point where it may well cost me pain—real pain—and some serious inconvenience.

The truly kind person is one who does not flinch at the cost of extending kindness. He forgets his own personal preferences to proffer help and healing to another. At the price of inconvenience, labor, and personal privation he goes out quietly and without fanfare to bring pleasure to another. Sensitive to the sorrow and suffering of a struggling society, he undertakes to do what he can to alleviate this suffering. He tries to make the world a better and brighter place for those enmeshed in its pain and pathos.

This is the quality of kindness that characterizes God our Father. He *does* care. He *does* suffer for us. Our Heavenly Father does come to us in absolute honesty and openness. He lays down His life for us, and He expends Himself without hesitation to enrich us. He identifies Himself with us in our dilemma. Utterly merciful, totally compassionate, incredibly self-giving, He has our welfare and well-being ever in mind—always.

In his second letter to the church of Corinth Paul put it this way: "For ye know the grace of our Lord Jesus Christ, that though he was rich, yet for your sakes he became poor, that ye through his poverty might be rich" (2 Cor. 8:9).

God's Great Kindness

Throughout the Scriptures the great theme of God's unrelenting kindness throbs like a powerful heartbeat. "His merciful kindness is great toward us . . ." (Ps. 117:2), is a refrain that never dies. It is repeated scores of times as a reminder that the mercy, compassion, and kindness of God flow to us freely, abundantly in refreshing rivers every day.

The kindness of God has drawn me to Him with bonds of love stronger than steel. The mercy of my Lord has endeared me to Him with enormous gratitude and thanksgiving. The generous compassion and intimate care of His Gracious Spirit are an enriching refreshment, new every day!

It is extremely difficult to convey on paper in human language, the incredible kindness of my Father, God. It seems to me that whoever attempts to do this always falls far short. This is a dimension of divine generosity that transcends our human capabilities to convey to one another. It can be experienced but it cannot be explained.

It is the kindness of God, expressed in Christ and revealed to us by His Spirit that supplies my salvation. His kindness makes provision for my pardon from sins and selfishness at the cost of His own laid down life. It is His kindness that forgives my faults and accepts me into His family as His dearly beloved child. His kindness enables me to stand acquitted of my wrongdoing, justified freely in His presence. God's kindness removes my guilt and I am at one with Him and others in peace. It is the kindness of God that enables Him to share Himself with me in the inner sanctuary of my spirit, soul, and body. His kindness enables me to be re-made, refashioned, re-formed gently into His likeness. His kindness gives enormous meaning and dignity to this life and endless delight in the life yet to come.

It is the constant, enduring, unchanging kindness of God that gives me every reason to rejoice and revel in life . . . all of life . . . this one and the next.

"Every good gift and every perfect gift is from above, and cometh down from the Father of lights, with whom is no variableness, neither shadow of turning" (James 1:17).

It is the kindness of God that enriches and energizes me not only spiritually but also morally and physically. I am surrounded on every side by the full-orbed environment of His overwhelming kindness. It comes flowing to me in a thousand forms from the fountainhead of His own love. All that I have and experience is an expression of His kindness.

And wonder of wonders—marvel of marvels—all of this in spite of my awkwardness, my waywardness, my stubborness, my perverseness. Nothing so pulverizes my pride and humbles my hard heart before Him.

Strange as it may seem, many people do not wish to either acknowledge or receive the kindness of God. In their arrogance and supposed self-sufficiency they naively and foolishly assume they are self-made individuals. They proudly proclaim their personal independence. Afraid somehow that they might be brought under obligation to Him, they don't want to be the recipients of God's kindness. They don't want the Divine Gardener interfering in the ground of their lives. So He who has bestowed on them life itself is kept at bay, or so they suppose. Little do they realize how they impoverish both themselves and Him.

A New Kind of Kindness

If, on the other hand, He is allowed to enter fully and freely into their experience some astonishing results will be produced. Perhaps the most pronounced will be the manner in which a new kind of kindness is generated.

I say this with great care, because kindness is not the exclusive fruit of Christian character. Some of the most moving kindness ever shown me came from total strangers, who, in some cases, were not Christians at all.

There is, however, one startling difference, and our Lord dealt with it in His majestic Sermon on the Mount in Matthew 5:43–48.

He points out that even pagans love those who love them, are courteous to those who can return the compliment, and extend kindness where kindness can be reciprocated.

But His advice to us is that our kindness should be of such a quality that we can even love our enemies, bless those that curse us, do good to those that hate us, pray for those who despise and persecute us. In so doing we demonstrate that we truly are His people.

Just as He bestows His good gifts on the godly and ungodly, and pours out His benefits on both believer and nonbeliever, He asks us to do likewise.

To live this way calls for courage. It means that some of those to whom we extend kindness will turn around and kick us in the teeth. It means that we will often be snubbed or scorned, and that our best intentions will sometimes be misunderstood and misconstrued.

When the good seed of God's own life germinates and takes root in the soil of our souls we give up our little games of playing tit-for-tat with others. No longer do we show love to get love back. No longer are we kind in order to be complimented and thought well of. We no longer give for what we can get. Those days are done—those tactics are terminated. Selfish self-satisfaction is no longer the mainspring of our actions.

The Gracious Side of Kindness

When God by His Gracious Spirit begins to produce the fruit of kindness in the garden of my character its thrust comes from the gracious generosity of His own goodness. He is kind because He cannot be otherwise. It is His essential nature. And likewise that becomes an integral part of my new nature bestowed by Him. It becomes part and parcel of my conduct, my character and conversation to just simply be kind—not for what I can get out of it, but because of what I can do for another.

It is sheer folly to extend kindness to others expecting that those same people will reciprocate. Often they will not show any appreciation at all. So unless our kindness is of divine origin we will end up deluded and discouraged. Rather, we should leave the results entirely in God's hands. It will surprise us to find that love, affection, appreciation, and kindness are bound to be returned to us, but often from totally unexpected sources and frequently from strangers to whom we never showed kindness in the first place.

God makes very sure that the principle of sowing and reaping never falters. And on the basis of His commitments to us we may be perfectly certain that any act or deed of kindness we show in mercy and compassion to another, will eventually be returned to us in rich and abundant compensation. We harvest what is planted. And when seeds of kindness are sown prayerfully in the garden plot of our lives we may be sure there will be a bountiful harvest of blessings for both us and others. Life can become exceedingly rich in benefits this way.

Kindness Embraces All of Life

Our kindness should be of such a caliber that it embraces all of life. It should enfold the pets in our care and the livestock on our farms. The shrubs, trees, grass, and flowers in our gardens—the forests, lakes, wildlife, and resources of the earth entrusted to our care—all should be treated with kindness. God in Christ by His Spirit is the Creator and supreme Conservationist. We are made in His likeness so we should do likewise.

Those who live with an active attitude of kindness, compassion, mercy, and concern for all of life are essentially persons of great inner light. There is a radiance and effulgence of enthusiasm and well-being about them. Warmth, affection, and good cheer emanate from them. It is the life and love of God apparent. This kindness dispels darkness, lifts loads, speaks peace, and inspires the downhearted.

Perhaps no other fruit of the Spirit has such far-reaching effects. It comes without display or ostentation, performing its sublime service almost in secret to slip away unseen. Yet its benefits remain to do their divine work in a weary old world.

I am ever reminded of the gentle and kindly David Livingstone. His tremendous foot safaris took him for thousands of miles through unmapped territory amongst strange and savage tribes. Yet wherever his footprints were left behind, there remained the legacy of the love of Christ expressed in his simple, humble kindness to the natives. Long after he was dead and gone to his "heavenly home," he was remembered in the dark continent as "the kind doctor." What greater accolade could any man earn?

Counterfeit Kindness

Before considering just how such kindness is produced in our characters one point should be made clear here about counterfeit kindness. Kindness and mercy are not an insipid, soft, sentimental indulgence. Nor is it tolerance of wrongs and evil in others.

For example, it is not kindness for a parent to allow a child to do wrong deliberately. It costs something to correct the misbehavior, both for parent and child. To overlook the wrong, to brush it aside, to sweep it under the carpet is not kindness. It is a distinct disservice.

It costs something to care.

There is suffering involved.

It is the kind physician who lances the boil, drains off the poison, cleanses the wound, and so restores the patient.

It is the charlatan who simply spreads salve over the sore while the ulcer does its deadly work beneath the surface.

So kindness entails courage, integrity, and selflessness.

The rather remarkable thing about this sort of kindness is that God puts an enormous priority upon it in His Word. Throughout the Scriptures we are told again and again that He looks for and expects kindness to be a hallmark of His people. It is one fruit that simply must be flourishing in the garden of our lives.

How then is it cultivated?

How does one set about encouraging this crop to take root and grow vigorously?

First of all we simply must recognize its importance—to God, to others, to ourselves. Much of God's good work in the world is achieved through mercy and compassion.

Kindness Is Caring

As His people we hold in our hands the happiness of others. The sense of self-worth, dignity, and personal esteem so essential to human well-being depends in large measure upon the kindness they receive from others.

We have it within our grasp to enrich the lives of our contemporaries by caring for them in a personal, meaningful, Christlike manner.

To do this takes time, lots of time. It cannot be done in a passing, flippant way. It is time-consuming (that is it uses up time we might otherwise spend on ourselves) to visit people, to make personal calls, to do little favors, to listen to the heart longings of others, to run errands for them, to help out with their work, to bear some of their burdens, to pray for them, to share their joys and sorrows, to write them letters, to give of our time and strength and means to them—to think of ways to brighten and cheer their lives.

Most of us are so terribly, terribly busy. It seems so often the ancient art of merely sitting quietly sharing an hour or two with another in gentle conversation has almost been lost.

Just last evening we invited an aged couple, ripe and mellow and sweet with long years of tough service for Christ, to share an evening with us in our little cottage. After a delicious dinner prepared with love and care by my wife we sat around a crackling fire of old fir knots that I had gathered from the hills in the afternoon.

The cheerful crackle of wood, the gentle warmth, the mellow mood of the room decorated with branches of scarlet sumac brought floods of peace and pleasure to the old people. In retrospect the elderly gentleman, his face aglow, reminisced about his boyhood on a Pennsylvania farm where he too used to go to the hills to gather pine knots for special festive occasions.

As the evening hours slipped away we shared books, pictures, art, and hearty laughs. Then my wife, who is only just learning the organ, offered to play for them. It set their spirits singing. To my amazement in a few minutes the elderly lady herself was seated at the instrument playing the organ for the first time in her life. This winter when we are away, our organ will be in their home to bring them hours of deep delight.

As they went out the door to go home, they were two people who for that evening had recaptured the joy of youth. Their eyes sparkled with gaiety and there was a lively vigor in their steps.

Kindness need not be anything grandiose or complicated. But it does take time and thought and love.

The second powerful, sure way to promote its production in our lives is to remind ourselves often of the great kindness of God to us.

It is my personal, unshakable conviction that when the Word of God instructs us clearly to spend time in communion with Christ, meditating upon His commands, it is primarily in connection with His mercy, compassion, and kindness to us. Anyone who reflects frequently on this will live and move in an atmosphere and attitude of humble gratitude to God. There will spring up constantly within the spirit a sublime sense of upwelling thanks and love for all the benefits bestowed by a loving Lord, the Gardener of his little life.

Under the compulsion and constraint of this love—this life of Christ poured into his own experience—he will go out gently to show kindness in a harassed and jaded old world.

Wherever he walks there will be left behind a legacy of love. For goodness and mercy will follow him all the days of his life.

TEN

Goodness—Grace and Generosity

Goodness might appear to be the most obvious fruit of God's Gracious Spirit. It is, however, also one of the most maligned and misunderstood.

In the original Anglo-Saxon, the very word "good'" carried the same connotation as "God." In fact, God was considered good. And good, in turn, was regarded as belonging essentially to God. It was just as valid to say "God is good" as it was to say "God is love."

Naturally from this it follows that "Love is good" in the same way that good is a facet of love being expressed. Goodness of this sort comes from God. He puts tremendous emphasis upon it. He extols it. When He was here amongst us it was reported in disarming simplicity that "He went about doing good."

The impact of that goodness moving with waves of irresistible impetus has swept across the centuries to encircle the globe, so that even today the goodness of Christ strikes us with enormous and far-reaching power. This goodness startles and astonishes us. It also stirs our sin-weary souls to their depths.

The World's Attitude toward Goodness

Yet in direct antithesis to the goodness of God the world often deprecates goodness. If they wish to belittle or deride one who seeks to serve God they call him a "do-gooder." The term "goody-goody" is one of the most malicious and hurtful that children hurl at one another. In the jargon of the world goodness is something insipid, weak, laughable, and to be despised.

In fact when our Lord was amongst us, even His good was evil spoken of by His antagonists. This is simply because good and evil are mutually exclusive. The goodness of God and the evil of the enemy are irresistibly opposed. The unrelenting antagonism between the two is the explanation for the chaos and unending carnage that characterizes human history. May I remind the reader, whoever you may be, that ultimately the goodness of God will prevail over evil. Love will overcome despair. Light will dispel darkness. Life will supplant death.

If this does not happen in the daily experience of your life here and now, ultimately it is bound to take place in the purposes of a good and loving God. It is He who has come amongst us as the Savior, to make this possible.

For God caused Christ, who himself knew nothing of sin, actually to be sin for our sakes, so that in Christ we might be made good with the goodness of God (2 Cor. 5:23, Phillips).

The cost of accomplishing this was so enormous that quite obviously goodness is a quality of God's character that most of us do not appreciate or value sufficiently. How often do we stand back in awe, overwhelmed, humbled, broken before Him because of His goodness? How often do we deliberately, determinedly, decisively beseech God to impart His goodness to us? How many of us really long above everything else to be made good with the goodness of God?

People will pray for love or joy, peace, patience, or kindness but seldom does one hear a heartrending cry coming from the depths of a sin-shattered, sin-stained, sin-sick soul—"O God, I just want to be made good!"

The True Nature of Goodness

The goodness of God is not some soft, spineless, sentimental indulgence of sensuality. It is not some passing mood of the moment that makes one "feel so good." It is not an emotional "high" in which reality fades away into some rosy glow of mystical magic.

Goodness is the rugged reality of God Himself coming to grips with the awfulness of sin. Goodness is that invincible power of God's own person overcoming evil. The goodness of God is the greatness of His love that dispels our despair and brings His life out of our death. The goodness of God is His generosity and graciousness in giving us Himself by His own Gracious Spirit. It is the enormous energy of His light and life extinguishing the evil in and around me.

This goodness is the pulsing, powerful performance of right in the midst of wrong all around us.

The truly great person is also a good person. And the really good person is always great. He is an individual of lofty ideals, noble purposes, strong character, reliable conduct, and trustworthy integrity. This is a tall order indeed. Few can claim all these credentials. Yet they were the most apparent, most obvious attributes of our Lord Jesus Christ.

This is why He was either so dearly loved or intensely hated. It was the goodness of God in His life that drew the common people like an irresistible magnet. But by the same dimension of divine goodness the superficially pious frauds were repelled. His goodness polarized people like steel filings in an electromagnetic field. They were either for or against Him.

The same will be true for anyone who truly follows Him. The Spirit of God moving strongly and energetically in anyone's experience polarizes those around him. Either they will be attracted or repelled by the goodness of God evident in the life.

God's Goodness and His Grace

This inherent goodness of God always moves hand in hand with the graciousness of God. In fact, we might say it is His grace which combined with His holiness (goodness, wholesomeness) makes it possible for us to be drawn to Him gently. His goodness is tempered by His grace. His goodness makes Him approachable.

It is the "good" Lord who is also so gracious to us. He draws near to us with infinite concern and compassion. Our Lord cares so deeply. He does not keep us at arm's length because of His unsullied goodness. Rather He comes running toward us, ready to throw His great, strong, warm arms of love around our sin-weary souls because of His gracious goodness.

He does not fawn upon us, nor does He flatter us. He does not indulge in flim-flam. He sees us in our sin and knows we are stained. Still he comes to grips with our sickened spirits.

As with the prodigal boy back from the pig-sty, there is a gold ring to go on the soil-stained hand; there is a white robe to clothe the sweat-stained body; there are fresh sandals for the dung-stained feet; there are kisses for the tear-stained cheeks.

Oh, the goodness of our God!

Oh, the graciousness of our Lord!

Oh, the generosity of our Christ!

These are the qualities of life exemplified by the goodness of God. They are what we mean when we say "God is good!"

Goodness Costs!

It costs a great deal to be good!

The price at which it comes is very high.

143

THE NINE FACETS OF GOD'S LOVE

A great part of that price is personal privation.

It takes a lot to be good and gracious and generous in a world where the mainstream of human thinking moves in the opposite direction.

Generosity that is so much a part of goodness is essentially a willingness to share what one has with another. This reaches out to embrace all of my life, not just my means. Generosity is much more than merely sending a handsome check to a charitable organization. It goes far beyond giving to others out of my surplus and my abundance.

When God, by His gracious Spirit, digs deeply in the soil of my soul He will implant there the new, divine impulse to be truly generous, truly self-giving.

This selfless self-sharing will entail more than just my money. He will put His finger upon my time, talents, interests, strength, energies, and capacities to enrich other lives. He will ask me to set aside my own selfish self-interest in order to give to others.

This is essentially what He did when He was here amongst us. There was never any desire for personal or private remuneration. All that He had and was, was poured out with open handed generosity to those whom He encountered. It was with enormous strength, dignity and self-control that He moved amongst men . . . crowds and mobs and multitudes of men and women. Yet ever and always He ministered to them either singly or collectively in goodness, graciousness, and generosity.

All that He had was theirs.

All He possessed was put at their disposal.

In genuine goodness He poured Himself out for people.

The Effect of Goodness

When the Spirit of God enters our little lives, there to shed abroad His love of which goodness is such an important part, we become changed people. It is the presence of Christ in the garden who alters and re-makes its entire character. We do in truth find that under the impact of His life and activity we are re-created. Fresh fruit—good fruit—grows in the garden.

> Therefore if any man be in Christ,
> he is a new creature (creation):
> old things are passed away:
> behold, all things are become new.
>   2 Cor. 5:17

There are three reasons for this. The first is that the guilt of the past is gone. Cleansed and forgiven by the enormous outpouring of God's own life in Christ, the person so freed from his past is liberated into a new life of positive, powerful goodness.

There is no sense of being bogged down in the morass of one's own wrongdoing. We are no longer polluted by the weeds and worries of our former wretched behavior. The ground of our souls has been cleaned up, set free from the fears and forebodings of our former life style.

The goodness which begins to emerge from the soil of our spirits is not our own but God's. We do not pretend to be pious. There is no longer any pretense or play acting. Instead simple, honest, sincere, genuine goodness becomes a supernatural outgrowth of the life of Christ within. Not forced or artificial, it is the simple expression of the gracious goodness of God's Spirit at work in me.

When this happens we discover that the second great attitude of graciousness toward others becomes apparent. We are not phony people perched up on little pedestals looking down with condescension upon our contemporaries. We are, rather, humble pilgrims on life's path, ready and eager to reach out to touch others struggling along life's tough trail beside us.

Any sense of pride or patronage toward others is gone. We know that but for the goodness of a loving God infinite in His grace toward us, we too might be down in the ditch of despair and degradation.

It is the good person, the gracious soul, the generous heart who helps the downtrodden. It is they who go out into a weary old world to bind up broken hearts, set the prisoners free, tend the sin-sick strangers, lift up the fallen, bring the oil of joy to those who mourn, spread light and cheer where darkness descends, feed the hungry, and share the good news of God's gracious love to the lost.

All of this can be done without show or ostentation. Goodness does not have to be publicized or paraded. It does not need a public relations program. Goodness is its own best advertisement.

The man or woman who expresses the genuine

goodness of a gracious God has nothing to fear, nothing to hide, nothing to protect. There is no need to apologize for his or her performance. It comes flowering like a fresh fruit blossom out of the divine life within, finding its final perfection in rich and ripe maturity of character like Christ's.

This caliber of character spontaneously gives rise to the third notable aspect of a re-made life, namely its generosity. These are the people—simple, open, uncomplicated people—who live with open faces, open hearts, and open hands.

In great good will they gladly share whatever they may possess with others. Spontaneously, happily, and with a touch of hilarity they give and give and give. Whatever they may own is simply held in open hands as a trust from their Heavenly Father. It is not theirs to grasp and gloat over greedily. It comes directly as a gift from God to be given away to others in need.

Whatever we may own, whether in large or small measure, when placed gladly in God's great strong hands can be blessed and multiplied a thousand times to enrich countless other lives. If clutched tightly and timidly to our own selfish souls it will shrivel away to a mere whimsy, wasted on oneself.

Genuine Goodness

It must be said here that the genuine goodness of God is totally distinct from the so-called "good works" done to gain merit.

The one springs directly from the in-dwelling Spirit of God. The other emerges from the selfish self-centeredness of one who seeks to be well spoken of by others. They are poles apart.

This latter self-righteousness is what our Lord deplored so vehemently amongst the haughty scribes, Sadducees and Pharisees. His most devastating denunciations were directed against the phony, pious pretense of these infamous "do-gooders." His most gracious and generous commendation was reserved for the despised Samaritan who showed true goodness to his neighbor.

How then does one become good with the goodness of God? Briefly, there are several simple measures that will produce this fruit.

1) Come to Calvary again. Spend time contemplating the cross. Read prayerfully the accounts of the crucifixion. Meditate quietly over the cost to God, in Christ, of our salvation. In the furnace of His affliction a titanic transaction took place. He was made sin that you and I might be made good with His own goodness. Accept His offer. Thank Him for it. Let Him bestow it on your broken heart. Allow Him to implant it in the stony soil of your soul. I have written of this at great length in my book *Rabboni.*

2) Cry out to Him to literally invade the territory of your little life. Ask Him to become the Good Gardener who will tend and care for your soul. Give Him liberty to love you, enfold you, cultivate you, and share His own life of gracious generosity with you. He will gladly pour Himself out upon you in tender loving care, so you in turn may do so to others.

3) As He lives in you and you in Him, keep the ground of your life clear, clean, and uncluttered. Confess quickly, in genuine sorrow, any sin or selfishness that might endanger His work within. Do not grieve His Gracious Spirit. Allow Him to have His way. Obey promptly, happily, simply, so that there will work out in your day-to-day conduct what he works in hour by hour. See Philippians 2:12–15.

4) Remind yourself *always* that you are the recipient, not the originator, of every gift, possession, and attribute you own. All come from Christ. Be deeply, genuinely grateful for His gracious generosity. In glad-hearted goodness go out to share His largess with a care-worn world. Let the impact of His goodness be passed on through you . . . to touch other seeking souls. *You will be surprised!*

ELEVEN

Faith and Faithfulness in Christians

Alongside of love itself, faith is the most frequently discussed facet of the Christian life. So much has been said and written about this subject that there is really nothing new or unusual that can be added here.

But it may surprise the reader to discover that faith, rather than being something distinct and apart from love, is in fact an integral part of it. Not only is faith bequeathed to the Christian believer as one of the fulsome fruits of God's own Gracious Spirit, but it is also bestowed as a special gift of God for the achievement of mighty exploits within the family of God (1 Cor. 12:9).

To fully understand faith that comes to us from Christ it is essential to remind ourselves once more that because it is a part of God's love, it is therefore a facet of selflessness. In other words, when faith is exercised in a person's conduct or behavior, selflessness is being demonstrated.

Faith by its very nature implies that I can see good in another outside myself.

This "good" may be either in God Himself, who as we discussed in the last chapter is goodness personified, or it may be in others around me.

This seeing, appreciating, and recognizing something of value and worth in another implies that I am reaching out of myself to touch the good in another. It means that I am no longer so self-centered or self-preoccupied that I see good only in myself as though I was the sole proprietor of good.

The simplicity of this concept may seem absurd to the reader. The subconscious response may well be, "Why of course there is bound to be some good in God and in others!" True enough. Why then are so many of us reluctant to respond to that good? Why do we hold back from giving ourselves to that good in glad freedom of spirit?

After all that is what faith is in action.

Faith is my deliberate and positive response to the good in another to the extent that I will act on his behalf in a personal, powerful way.

This activity on my part means that I am fully prepared to invest something of myself in another. It means that I am willing to share my life along with all its capacities (time, strength, attention, talents, means, energy, affection, acceptance) with another. It means that I actively, energetically give of my best to another outside of and apart from myself.

To speak of faith in any other way than this is to indulge in mere "believism." It is to play around with pious platitudes that pack no punch at all. This sort of superficial spirituality is actually the great bane of Christianity. Literally hundreds of thousands of people claim they trust in God; they claim to have faith in Christ; they claim to be believers, yet their lives and personal conduct are a denial and travesty of true faith.

The reason for this assertion is the obvious and devastating lack of genuine faith everywhere. When our Lord lived amongst us He was continually looking for this dynamic trust and response to Himself. Whenever He found even the tiniest fragment of faith being exercised in Him He was delighted. Over and over He remarked joyfully that here and there amongst the most unlikely individuals living, viable faith was active.

The Source of Faith

This faith of God's Gracious Spirit can spring only from the fountain source of God's own generous love shed abroad in our lives. Having its source in Him, it flows freely to us. It becomes active in our innermost being, then flows out in our self-giving back to Him and others.

This is what the author of the epistle to the Hebrews meant when He declared unequivocally in chapter 12:2, "(We look) unto Jesus the author and finisher of our faith."

153

This faith is the facet of God's love which finds me giving myself to others in faithfulness, fidelity, and unyielding loyalty. It expresses itself in a constant yet continuous investment of all that I am and own in both God and men. I believe in them to the point where I am prepared to pour my life into them.

Now if we want to see this caliber of conduct in bold relief, we do not look at men or women. We look at God Himself. The faith of God finds its fullest and most sublime expression in His faithfulness to us mortals.

Just as His love, kindness, patience, and goodness emanate from Him in an eternal, unending stream of benevolence to us, so His great faithfulness flows to us undiminished every day. It simply cannot be otherwise because of who He is.

The Word of God abounds with divine declarations about the faithfulness of God. Just as an example in Psalm 36:5–9 inspired by God's Spirit David, the great poet-singer of Israel, exults:

Thy mercy, O Lord, is in the heavens;
and thy faithfulness reacheth unto the clouds.

Thy righteousness is like the great mountains;
Thy judgments are a great deep: O Lord,
thou preservest man and beast.

How excellent is thy lovingkindness,
O God! therefore the children of men
put their trust under the shadow of thy wings.

They shall be abundantly satisfied with
the fatness of thy house;

And thou shalt make them drink
of the river of thy pleasures.

For with thee is the fountain of life:
in thy light shall we see light.

It is legitimate and appropriate to ask, how can
God very God, He who is righteous and impeccable
in character, deign to have faith in us feeble, frail
human beings with all our foibles and follies? How
can He who so transcends our tiny mortal lives with
the greatness of His eternal goodness be faithful to
us? Why does He even bother to bestow Himself
and all His benefits upon us? How can He be so
gracious, generous, and good to share Himself with
unpredictable people who in turn are so often un-
faithful—either to Him or one another?

These are indeed sobering and searching questions.

If we take them seriously and ponder them privately in the seclusion of our own spirits they will
humble us.

There are two simple answers:

The Nature of God Himself

The first and foremost is His own inherent righteousness, justice, integrity, and holiness. So wholesome, so good, so selfless is our God that He cannot
be anything but faithful. He is that way because
that is His very makeup.

If for no other reason, *He must inevitably be faithful
(true) to Himself.* He is very truth, hence He cannot
act except in utter good faith. This being so it ex-

plains why He comes to us in good will, with peace, eager and anxious to pour this same attribute of His own character into our little lives. He yearns to share this self-giving capacity with us selfish, self-centered people. With profound longing He waits to see this fruit of His own Spirit spring to life in us. He waits patiently to see it ripen and mature into active, living faith of obedience that is reciprocated back to Him and out to others.

The reason He is prepared to do all this is not what we may be initially ("There is none that doeth good, no, not one"—Ps. 14:3. "For all have sinned and come short of the glory [character] of God"—Rom. 3:23), *but what we may become. He sees within us the capacity to be conformed to His own character.* He who made us knows that under the impulse of His own Gracious Spirit, and the divine direction of His own living Word we can become His sons and daughters, adopted into His family, maturing into the very likeness of Christ.

This is not theoretical theology. It is not just divine doctrine. It does happen in human hearts and lives. We can be re-born. We can be re-created. We can be made into men and women, whose character, conduct, and conversation are like Christ's (see 2 Cor. 5:15–17).

And because all this is possible He finds joy in being faithful to us. He is confident of what He can achieve and accomplish working in the garden of our little lives. He can tear out the old brambles and briars; He can clear the ground of rocky unbelief; he can break up the hard-packed paths; He can open us up to receive the good seed of His own winsome Word.

This He does with unfailing good will and unending faithfulness. Initially God made man in love, chosen before ever planet earth was formed, to become His own dear children. And though humanity has been blighted and devastated by sin and evil, He alone knew that because of His faithfulness to His own creation, light could drive back the darkness; life could vanquish death; love could dispel despair; and faith (His faith) could displace our unfaithfulness.

All of this stirs my spirit to its depths. It enlivens my confidence in Christ and quickens the response of my soul to His overtures. It generates within the garden of my life a climate and condition conducive to genuine faith. I begin to see that because He is faithful to me, I in turn can be faithful to Him and others. Because He first loved me it is possible in turn for me to love (1 John 4:4–19).

The immediate result of such faith becoming evident is that God Himself is delighted. The Scriptures state unequivocally that without faith it is impossible to please God (Heb. 11:6).

When by the positive response of my whole person I actually determine to do what He asks of me: when in quiet, simple confidence I comply with His will and wishes: when gladly, freely I give myself and what I have to him: when I deliberately invest myself in His enterprises knowing that my life can be spent in no better way, God is delighted. He has found faith. He has a crop of trust, loyalty, and fidelity springing up in the field of my life that He has tilled and tended with such diligence and faithfulness. Are we surprised that He should be ecstatic?

Faith's Impact on Others

The second great result of faith beginning to flourish in us is the impact it has upon our contemporaries. In spite of the unpredictable character and conduct of people we begin to look for the good in them. In spite of their fickle ways and foolish behavior we begin to believe in them. In spite of their human failures and foibles we start to see them as God our Father does. We look at them the way our Lord looks at them, and begin to see as the Spirit of God sees. His love is being shed abroad in our hearts, so now we can discover and discern the potential locked up in people. Our faith is not in their peculiarities but in their possibilities. With faith we believe and know and are assured that under God they can become great and noble.

Faith active in this way produces miracles in those around us. Such faith puts the best construction on every situation and looks for the silver edge on every dark cloud. It searches for any hint of honor and dignity. It believes that with God, all things are possible. It pushes on, perseveres, remains loyal in spite of reverses and disappointments. Such faith is steadfast in spite of shaking experiences and has its gaze fastened upon Him who is faithful, not upon the chaos and confusion of circumstances around us.

It is in the atmosphere of this confidence in Christ that the faithful person (a person full of faith) quietly carries on living in serenity, strength, and stability. He is not shaken by the stormy events or unpredictable behavior of others around him. Gently, calmly, without fanfare he simply gives and gives and gives himself to God and others. This he does in a hundred unobtrusive little ways wherein his life is poured out, laid out, on behalf of them because he really does "believe in them" and in what God can do.

In his classic essay on God's love, *The Greatest Thing in the World,* Henry Drummond deals with this concept in moving language: "You will find, if you think for a moment, that the people who influence you are people who believe in you. In an atmosphere of suspicion men shrivel up; but in that atmosphere they expand, and find encouragement and educative fellowship. It is a wonderful thing that here and there in this hard, uncharitable world there should still be left a few rare souls who think no evil. This is the great unworldliness. Love 'thinketh no evil,' imputes no motive, sees the bright side, puts the best construction on every action. What a delightful state of mind to live in! What a stimulus and benediction even to meet with it for a day! To be trusted is to be saved. And if we try to influence or elevate others, we shall soon see that success is in proportion to their belief of our belief in them. For the respect of another is the first restoration of the self-respect a man has lost; our ideal of what he is becomes to him the hope and pattern of what he may become."

This faith moves mountains of inertia and perverseness in other people. It pulverizes prejudices and impossibilities. This faith is the fruit of God's Gracious Spirit that sweetens a sour world. It replaces suspicion and distrust with friendship and hope and good cheer. It makes our friends, family, and casual acquaintances stand tall. It turns the cynic and skeptic from cynicism to salvation.

Sad to say there simply is not much of this faith abroad in the world. In fact it is becoming a rather rare attribute. It matters not where we look for it— in the home, between families, in business, in the church, amongst nations or between individuals. The virtues of deep loyalty, mutual trust, fidelity, and consistent faithfulness, which are all part and parcel of faith in action, are rapidly diminishing in society. It is not the least surprising that our Lord asked the question: "When the Son of man cometh, shall he find faith on the earth?" (Luke 18:8).

Faith is or is not apparent and present to the same degree that selflessness is. It is really that simple. If people are preoccupied with only their own self-centered self-interests then love (the love of God) with its attendant attribute of faith simply does not function.

On the other hand, when faith is active it affects all of life. We see ourselves as stewards entrusted with time, talents, means, and concern to be used on behalf of God and our fellow men. We are entrusted with enormous responsibilities which can benefit and enrich the generation of which we are a part. We are required to be faithful stewards of all that has been put at our disposal for the uplift and encouragement of our contemporaries. It is our privilege and pleasure to give ourselves and share what we have with a world in deep distress. This is all an integral and practical part of living faith in action.

Faith of this caliber comes from God. If we lack it we must ask for it. He urges us to come boldly requesting good gifts from Him (Luke 11:9–13). He does bestow His Gracious Spirit on those who request His presence and are prepared to cooperate wholeheartedly with His commands (Acts 5:32). He will not withhold any good thing from those who seek His faith in sincerity. He is faithful!

As we see this faithfulness demonstrated to us daily in a thousand different ways by a loving Father it will increase and fortify our faith in Him. Likewise it will motivate us to go out and have faith in our fellow pilgrims on life's rocky roads. We will come alongside to help lift their loads, cheer their spirits, and inspire their souls.

Faith of this sort comes from a clear conscience. If our view of God in Christ is clear and uncluttered, our estimation of others is not dimmed or distorted. We see our responsibilities to both God and man clearly. Accordingly we act in good faith. Allowing nothing to come between us and others, we walk in the light as He is in the light, faithful always.

In every situation that arises we count on the vigilant, faithful presence of God Himself to guide and empower us in our decisions and demeanor. He who said, "Lo, I am with you always, even unto the end of the age," will be faithful to Himself, to His Word, and to us.

TWELVE

Humility— Meekness and Gentleness

In the rough and tumble of our abrasive twentieth century, humility is scarcely considered a virtue. Such qualities as meekness and gentleness are not the sort that most people seek in order to succeed. We are a fast-moving, masterful, permissive people who from the cradle (if there are still cradles) learn to shove and push and scream and scramble to get ahead—to plant our proud feet on the top of the totem pole.

Fiercely we contend for our rights, believing the strange philosophy that to be big and bold and brazen is best. We subscribe to the idea that since no one else will blow my horn for me, I must blow my own bugle loudly and long. We are completely convinced that unless we make our own mark in the world we will be forgotten in the crush—obliterated from memory by the milling masses around us.

From the hour we begin to take our first feeble, frightened steps as tiny tots we are exhorted to "stand on your own feet." We are urged and encouraged to "make it on your own." We are told to "make your own decisions." We are stimulated to be aggressive, self-assertive, and very self-assured. All of these attributes we are sure will lead to ultimate greatness.

In the face of all this it comes to us as a distinct shock to hear our Lord declare: "Whosoever therefore shall humble himself as this little child, the same is greatest in the kingdom of heaven" (Matt. 18:4).

Somehow in our society humility and greatness are thought to be mutually exclusive. Consequently many Christians are confronted on this point with the necessity of making some sort of mental, emotional or volitional adjustments. Where does truth lie here? Who has the secret of success? Does one adopt the view of contemporary culture or the rather unpalatable proposition of Jesus Christ who stated without hesitation, "Let him who would be greatest amongst you be your servant"?

First Corinthians 13:4, 5 states bluntly that charity (love) "vaunteth not itself, is not puffed up, doth not behave itself unseemly, seeketh not her own."

The selfless, self-effacing character of God's love simply does not permit it to strut and parade itself pompously. It will have no part of such a performance. It is not proud, arrogant, puffed up with its own importance.

The Essence of Humility

This quality of life that produces genuine humility in the human spirit bestows upon us a truly balanced view of ourselves and others. We see the greatness and goodness in our God and in others around us. Likewise it enables us to see ourselves as we really are. We see our own relative insignificance in the great mass of mankind, yet we also see we are of great worth to Christ who has called us from darkness into the light of His own love. We see ourselves as sinners, yet at the same time those who have been saved from their despair to become the sons of God.

So it is the generosity of our God, the kindness of Christ, the patient perseverance of His Holy Spirit drawing us to Himself that humbles our haughty hearts. It is the depth of Christ's compassion which crumbles the tough crust that accumulates around our self-centered characters. The inflowing impartation of His own gentle, gracious Spirit displaces our own arrogance and self-preoccupation. It leaves us laden with His own fruits of lowliness and gentleness.

There is an old saying among orchardists that "The most heavily laden branches always bow the lowest on the tree." It is likewise true in human conduct.

Meekness not Weakness

Meek men are not weak men. The meek are gracious, congenial individuals who are easy to get along with. These genial, good-natured souls win friends on every side because they refuse to shove, push, and throw their weight around. They do not win their wars with brutal battles and fierce fights. They win their way into a hundred hearts and homes with the passport of a lowly, loving spirit.

Their unique genius is their gentleness. This quality of life does not come from a position of feeble impotence, but rather from a tremendous inner strength and serenity. Only the strong, stable spirit can afford to be gentle. It is the sublime Spirit of the living God who bestows upon us the capacity to express genuine concern and compassion for others. His selfless self-giving enables us to treat others with courtesy and consideration. This quality is much more than a thin veneer of proper proprietry or superficial politeness.

This caliber of humility, meekness, and gentleness comes at great cost. It is not a mere convenience that we use to accommodate our own selfish ends. Rather, it is the epitome of a laid-down life, poured out, laid out, lived out on behalf of others.

The Meekness of God in Christ

If we are to see this humility, this condescension, this meekness at its best we must look at the life of our Lord. In a few short, stabbing, stunning verses it has been summed up for us in Philippians 2:1–11.

Look not every man on his own things,
but every man also on the things of others.

Let this mind be in you,
which was also in Christ Jesus:

Who, being in the form of God,
thought it not robbery to be equal with God:

but made himself of no reputation,
and took upon him the form of a servant,
and was made in the likeness of men:

and being found in fashion as a man,
he humbled himself,
and became obedient unto death,
even the death of the cross.

Wherefore God also hath highly exalted him,
and given him a name which is above every name.
(Phil. 2:4–9).

Such enormous condescension and self-giving stills our spirits in His presence. What lengths He went to become identified with us struggling mortals in the morass of our sins! O the depths to which He descended to deliver us from our dilemma of despair! What humiliation He undertook deliberately to rescue and redeem us from the enemy of our souls!

Yes, it costs a great deal to experience and know true humility. For most people its price is prohibitive. They simply will not pay it. There is a real "buyer's resistance" to the cost of gentleness and meekness amongst us.

We simply do not wish to become of "no reputation."

We want no part of playing "the suffering servant."

We refuse to become "doormats" on whom others wipe their feet without compunction.

We are not excited by involvement with the weak and woebegone.

We are not attracted by the "Man of Sorrows." There is nothing glamorous about this One. Like so many others we tend to despise and reject such submissiveness.

The consequence is that in the garden of our lives there springs up a mixed crop of fruit and weeds. On the one hand there are places where pride, self-assertion, arrogance, self-indulgence, and abrasive aggressiveness mark our behavior. These often tend to overwhelm the more gentle fruits of God's Gracious Spirit. They climb all over them, almost choking them out completely.

Unless we keep clearly in view the life and character of Christ we will succumb to the eternal temptation of living like our contemporaries—giving tit for tat, insisting on our rights, demanding our pound of flesh, stepping on anyone who trespasses against us, while all the time pushing for prominence and recognition. This is the world's way. Christ calls us to tread in His footsteps. He tells us to deny ourselves daily (give up our rights to ourselves). He asks us to take up our cross continuously (that which cuts diametrically across my selfish self-interest), crossing out the great "I" in my life to produce peace.

None of this is very appealing.
It goes against the grain of our old nature.
It is not a bit glamorous or romantic.

The Benefits of Meekness

Yet its fruitage has three fantastic benefits which escape most people. Here they are:

1) Humility is the only seedbed from which faith can spring. The pompous, proud, self-assured soul sees no need for God or others in his/her life. Such people will "make it on their own," they believe naively. They have faith only in themselves. They end up disillusioned, self-centered, lonely, and mocked by their own self-pity.

In brokenness and contrition the humbled person cries out to God for help. He reaches out to Christ for restoration and healing. He exercises faith in another because he knows he must touch someone greater than himself. Similarly he seeks out others he can serve and in his suffering service finds fulfillment and freedom from himself.

2) It is to such souls that God gives Himself gladly, freely. He draws near to those who draw near to Him. He delights to dwell with those of a broken and contrite spirit. "The Lord is nigh unto them that are of a broken (humbled) heart; and saveth such as be of a contrite (meek) spirit" (Ps. 34:18).

The reason for this is so self-evident most of us almost miss it. God, who is selfless love, can only feel at home and be in harmony with the person who is likewise selfless. Here there can be no friction. All is at peace. All is well.

In vivid and shattering contrast we are warned explicitly that God actually resists the proud. He does not just tolerate or indulge arrogant souls. He actually opposes them actively. This is a terrifying truth that should make any self-centered, haughty individual tremble (see James 4:4–10).

How appalling to realize that in our pride we are being diametrically resisted by our selfless, self-giving God. This is inevitable because the two are mutually exclusive and eternally opposed to one another.

What a dreadful discovery to find that instead of going through life being helped by God, we are in fact struggling along "hindered" by Him. Are we surprised we don't succeed?

3) In contrast to this the third amazing reality about humility is the impact it makes upon our fellow men.

It is the genuinely humble, gentle soul who wins friends and draws around him a circle of loving associates. This quality of life draws others as surely as nectar in a blossom attracts bees.

The gentle, genial person is the recipient of affection. People bestow on him their blessings. He is lavished with love and surrounded with compassion. And wherever he goes hearts and homes are flung open with a warm welcome to his winsome presence.

The proud, arrogant, haughty person has few if any friends. He stands upon his little pedestal of pride in grim and gaunt loneliness. Others leave him alone. They ignore him deliberately. If he is so independent let him live his own life; let him go his own way; let him suffer the agony of his own selfishness.

Humility Is an Everyday Affair

In my wallet I carry a faded, yellow newspaper clipping that has traveled around the world with me for nearly 30 years. It reads: "The old order may change, giving place to new, but there are a few fundamentals that remain with us as time goes by." A reader has sent me an excerpt from a book entitled *Quite a Gentleman*, written 100 years ago.

It stated, "Here's a list of little marks by which we may single out a gentleman from the common crowd: He is particular about trifles, answers his letters promptly, is quick to acknowledge a kindness, thankful for small mercies, never forgets to pay a debt nor to offer an apology that is due. He is punctual, neat, doing everything he undertakes as thoroughly and as heartily as possible."

The reader may well ask, "What has punctuality got to do with being a gentleman?" or "What has answering letters promptly got to do with love and the fruit of God's Spirit called gentleness?"

Let me explain. When all is said and done the fruits of God's Gracious Spirit must find expression in the simple, down-to-earth conduct of our everyday lives. They are not just theory or theology.

The person who is invariably late is demonstrating by his action that he does not care if he inconveniences another. He is saying not in words but in

171

his behavior, "My time is more important than yours! You can wait! Your time can be wasted. It is of no consequence!" Here we see selfish, self-centered pride and arrogance actually being acted out toward another in brazen behavior. This is the antithesis of the love of God.

The person who is irresponsible about replying to letters is equally selfish. The common excuses are a dead giveaway. "I didn't have time. I was too busy. I just didn't get around to it." Note the prominence of I in the picture. In so many words these people are saying, "It doesn't matter to me how long you have to wait. I don't care if you are worried and wonder what is happening. I'm so busy taking care of myself there really is no time to spare for you. I don't really feel responsible for your peace of mind."

Too many of us have the idea that somehow the fruits of God's Spirit are some mystical, magical, superspiritual effulgence that flows into our emotions and minds moving us to be superspiritual people. This is not so.

The fruits of God's Spirit are sown in the soil of my soul and spirit by His Spirit. And what He works in, I must then proceed to work out. What God impresses upon me as being proper and appropriate I have an obligation to carry out. We are not plaster-cast saints.

As people who deliberately decide and determine to do God's will, we set ourselves to comply with His wishes. We set our wills to seek His face—to serve others and to deny ourselves. There is a cost to consider—a price to pay. There is a death to self to endure daily.

If we need stimulation and inspiration to so live a laid-down life we need look in but one direction to find it—to Him who loved us and gave Himself for us.

> Hereby perceive we the love of God,
> because he laid down his life for us:
> and we ought to lay down our lives for
> the brethren (John 3:16).

It is a straightforward case of cause and effect, not some complicated formula or technique. In fact, not until the impact of the laid-down life of Christ comes crashing through the crust around our hard, self-centered hearts will humility ever displace our despicable self-preoccupation. Then and only then will the expulsive power of humility's presence displace our selfishness enabling us to go out into a broken, shattered, bleeding, wounded world as suffering servants.

The humility of Christ, the meekness of His Gracious Spirit, the gentleness of our God can only be known, seen, felt, and experienced by a tough world in the lives of God's people. If the society of our twentieth century finds God at all they will have to find Him at work in the garden of His children's lives. It is there His fruits should flourish and abound. It is there they should be readily found.

As we contemplate and meditate over the gracious generosity of God in Christ, humbling Himself on our behalf, it should warm our cold hearts and flood them with the warmth of His love. Out of an enormous, overflowing, spontaneous sense of thanks and gratitude we should be able to go out and live before others in humility and gentleness, serving them in sincerity and genuine simplicity. As the Father sent the Son into the world, so He in turn sends us out to serve a sick society.

This we can do without pomp or pretext. This we can do walking humbly, quietly, gently with our God. It may astound and amaze a skeptical society. After all, it isn't the norm. It won't win applause or accolades. But it may very well win some for the Savior.

This is no soft life to live. But it is the restful way. It is the peaceful way. It is the best way. It is His way!

> Come unto me, all ye that labour
> and are heavy laden, and I will
> give you rest.
>
> Take my yoke upon you, and learn of me;
> for I am meek and lowly in heart:
> and ye shall find rest unto your souls.
>
> For my yoke is easy, and my burden is light
> (Matt. 11:28 –30).

THIRTEEN

Self-control (Control of Self): Temperance -Moderation

Self-control, temperance, moderation, self-restraint are all terms used to define the last of the nine fruits of the Spirit listed in Galatians 5:22, 23. To put it in the terminology of 1 Corinthians 13:1–7 the phrases, "Doth not behave itself unseemly," or "Does not act in an inappropriate or unbecoming manner," are used.

This sounds so simple and somewhat dignified, but it is so very, very difficult to do in actual life.

Self-control may be the last facet of God's love in the list, but that certainly does not reduce it to the least important.

No doubt it is true and fair to say that it is one aspect of Christian conduct and character and conversation with which most of us have the greatest difficulty. Of all the fruits which should flourish in the garden of our lives this may well be the one which is the most "spotty," "uneven," and "irregular."

In some situations we behave in a most exemplary and commendable manner. At other times we behave worse than beasts. There are days when we seem to act in decent and dignified ways. On other occasions we can become erupting volcanoes of venom and violent vituperation. If we are earnestly honest with ourselves we discover that there is too often, as James puts it so forcefully, both sweet and saline water springing up from the same inner fountain. Or to use our Lord's metaphor, the ground of our personalities produces both grapes and wild brambles, figs and thistles.

Consistency and credibility are so often not apparent. As the prophet of old put it in such poignant poetry, the good husbandman came to his garden looking for sweet fruit and found instead only wild, sour grapes:

> Now will I sing to my well-beloved a song of my beloved touching his vineyard. My well-beloved hath a vineyard in a very fruitful hill: and he fenced it, and gathered out the stones thereof, and planted it with the choicest vine, and built a tower in the midst of it, and also made a winepress therein: and he looked that it should bring forth grapes, and it brought forth wild grapes (Isa. 5:1, 2).

Such fruit sets one's teeth on edge.

Stating it in rather simple layman's language we would say that instead of being people who do God's will, who speak His words and work His works in the world, we frequently find ourselves outside His control, living out our own strong-willed, wayward ways.

The Character of Self-Control

What, then, do the Scriptures mean when they speak of self-control? What is true temperance? What is the meaning of genuine moderation in a man's life? Is it possible of production? Can it be cultivated? Or is this one of those fickle fantasies that eludes us in our everyday experiences where we encounter a thousand temptations to cast off all restraint and live life to the hilt?

Before answering these questions one thing must be made clear. This so-called "self-control" is not the worldling's concept of being a stoic. It is not being a stern spartan. The picture here is not the grim, rigid idea of setting the jaw, steeling the will to endure life with cold cynicism. It is not a case of "grin and bear it." Self-control for God's person does not imply that with severe self-discipline I can control my conduct.

No, no, no! The answer does not lie there.

Self-control for the Christian means that my "self," my whole person, my whole being, body, soul, spirit comes under the control of Christ. It means that I am an individual governed by God. My entire life, every aspect of it—whether spiritual, moral or physical—has become subject to the sovereignty of God's Spirit. I am a "man under authority." The running of my affairs, my attitudes, my actions is a right which has been relinquished and turned over to God's Gracious Spirit.

To use the word picture of a garden, the "Good Gardener" has come through the gate. The ground of my entire being is His to do with as He wishes. It is His privilege to produce what He wills in the way He desires without hindrance. He it is who alone has the right to control the crop production. It is He who decides what shall be done in every area of this garden.

Christ—One in Control

If we wish to see this kind of control at its best we do not look at other human beings. Even the choicest Christians are sometimes speckled birds. The best of men have feet of clay. The sweetest saints can sometimes turn sour.

Instead we look at God Himself. We see Him best in Christ. When He was here amongst us He stated unflinchingly, "He that hath seen me hath seen the Father" (John 14:9).

It was this One who repeatedly asserted that He was completely under divine control. He came, not to do His own will, but His Father's. The words He spoke were not His, but the Father's. The works He carried out were God's own enterprises. Because of this "inner control" He in return was in control of every situation He faced.

Wherever Christ moved, whomever He met, whatever circumstances He encountered, the remarkable aspect of His life was that He was always in control. He was never taken unawares, never caught in a crisis. Jesus was never manipulated, nor was He ever at the mercy of the mob. Even during those desperate, diabolical last hours from the time of His betrayal until His battered body hung on a cruel Roman cross, He moved in quiet strength, enormous dignity, and majestic might. Before the Pharisees, the Sadduccees, the scribes, even Judas His betrayer, the high priests, the Sanhedrin, cunning King Herod, the political opportunist Pilate, the brutal Roman soldiers, the blood-thirsty mobs of Jerusalem, Jesus of Nazareth, the Christ of God, was supremely in control.

And this was because He was God-controlled.

I have written at great length on this theme in *Rabboni*. It will not be elaborated here.

But it must be said with great emphasis that if some of us wonder why our lives are such a tangle; if we wonder why we seem to live in an inner jungle; if the soil of our souls seems to be buried beneath a bramblelike growth of unchecked, uncontrolled wild vines, it is because we have not allowed ourselves to be brought under the control of the Good Gardener.

We simply don't want Him interfering in the grounds of our lives. We prefer to go our own way, to carve out our own careers, to do our own thing, to grow our own sour grapes, to live lost in the briars and brambles of self-determination. In our stupidity we seem to think we can control our own destiny only to discover that our lives are *unmitigated disasters*.

Yet I would pause here momentarily to remind the reader that despite our willful waywardness God does not write us off as a total loss. He does not dismiss us in disgust, nor does He deal with us in a diatribe against our sins. He does not reward us with abuse and malignancy according to our iniquities. Read Psalm 103.

If He did, where would I be?

Rather He comes to me in His own gracious, generous, gentle self-control, offering to move quietly into the turmoil of my soul and there take control. He longs to be given the chance to govern me as God, very God. He is eager to bring order out of the inner chaos of my character. He, the Christ of God, comes to me willing to become my Lord, my Master, my King, who alone can adequately control the untamed territory of my life. He, the Gracious Spirit of the Living God, will gladly enter the ground of my being to there exercise His own superb sovereignty in such a way that His purposes for me as His person are realized.

In all of this there is tremendous hope.

The control of my self is more than mere wishful thinking. It can happen. It can become increasingly the norm for life.

Controlled by Christ

My whole spirit, its intuition, conscience, and communion with Christ can come steadily under the control of God's own Gracious Spirit. My total personality—mind, emotions and will—can be at

Christ's command. My entire body—its appetites, drives, desires, and instincts—can be governed by God. It is possible to live a godly life of moderation and temperance in testing times.

But there is a price to pay.

Inner peace and outer strength come at high cost. Righteousness, rightness in our relationships to God, others, and ourselves is not a "run of the mill" product. It doesn't just come about by happenstance. The manner in which a man is changed from the old, erratic life of wild and untamed behavior to one of stability and serenity is pretty severe.

It means giving up my rights. It goes beyond daydreaming about being a delightful sort of soul. It gets down to the grass roots where I relinquish my self-rule and turn myself over irrevocably to God.

In a book of this sort it is not intended to go into all the ramifications of what such a total relinquishment might entail. Each of us soon discovers those areas in which we have not turned over the territory to God for His absolute control.

But at least I will deal briefly with the soul: i.e. my mind, emotions, will (disposition).

Our minds and imaginations can be monsters. We can allow them to literally monopolize our entire outlook on life. Our thought patterns can become so set against that which is good that even God Himself does not enter our thought life. He is excluded from the reasoning we do or the vain and sometimes vicious imaginations we indulge in. Pride and self-preoccupation are the pompous rulers of our minds. All our days and even some of our dreams are devoted to selfish aims and ambitions. God's Gracious Spirit really has no input into our thinking.

Yet the Word of God makes it clear that our thoughts, minds, and imaginations should and must all be transformed and renewed (Rom. 12:1–3). We are not capable of self-improvement in this way. It is a case of deliberately turning over this terrain in the garden of our lives to God. He is the one who will come in to effect the change. He can alter the direction of our minds.

A Prayer of Submission

It is proper and appropriate to request verbally and audibly, "O Christ, here I am with my tumultuous thoughts and rampant imagination. I turn them over to You. Take them under Your control. Invade this territory of my being. Lay claim to this chunk of grievous ground. I give it to You for Your government. Manage it. Think Your thoughts through me. Concentrate my interest in Yourself. Center my attention on that which is beautiful, true, worthwhile, and noble! Remake me as you desire!"

This is not a simple, easy petition to make in earnest.

The monster of my mind may well contest such a request.

But if in total, genuine, sincere relinquishment this is done the results are bound to be beautiful. Christ will take control.

It must be said here unequivocally that any area of my being deliberately, sincerely and wholeheartedly turned over to the control of Christ, He will take. This does not mean there will always be sudden and dramatic changes. But it does guarantee that gradually there will be a gentle growth in godliness. The growing of fruit and flowers does not happen in a day. The process is a slow but steady unfolding of the blossom, the formation of the fruit, and at last its beautiful ripening. Luscious purple grapes are not produced in one week nor does a gracious mind mature in a moment.

In the realm of our emotions the need for the Spirit's control is absolutely imperative. Apart from His Gracious Presence our inner feelings can be terrible tyrants. Because of the never-ending ebb and flow of our interrelationship with other human beings the tensions produced by unpredictable people make life a complex maze.

In very truth we simply never know what new and difficult dilemmas a day may bring. We find ourselves interacting with strange people and new circumstances. Our actions and reactions too often are governed not by God but by our own selfish self-interest. We may be entertaining all sorts of abhorrent inner attitudes to protect our pride, position or property. These may or may not find expression in hostility, anger, criticism, bitterness, jealousy, hatred or a score of other more subtle feelings and emotions.

As God's people this sort of performance is not acceptable. In Galatians 5, and even more clearly in Romans 8, we are warned and alerted to the formidable fact that such behavior is in truth the wild, bitter fruit of our old self-life. These are called "the works of the flesh" (Gal. 5:19–21). They are the exact antithesis of the fruits of God's Spirit.

Those who produce such attitudes quite obviously are not under the control of Christ. They are not being governed by God, nor are they subject to the sovereignty, the direction, the leading of His Spirit.

As Christians we do not live under the tyranny of our temperaments. We live by faith in Christ's capacity to control our tempestuous emotions.

Just as with our minds, so with our feelings. These must be put at God's disposal definitely and deliberately. A prayer as earnest as that made for the mind is appropriate here:

"O Gracious God, life is too complex, too full of tensions and turmoil for me to cope alone. I so easily lose control of myself. My emotions are prone to such perversion. Like a wild, unchecked growth they soon smother out the good growth of Your planting. Move in mightily and take over my whole temperament. Tame my inner turmoil. Water me with Your presence. Let me know You are here. Do that within me which I cannot do myself. Empower me to love and live and lay down my 'self' as You did when You were walking the dusty trails of this tired old world. May my feelings become a garden of refreshment for Yourself and those who meet me."

The Christ-Controlled Will

Then there is the realm of my will. This is the central citadel of my disposition. It is where the deep, permanent decisions of my volition are decided. I have written at great length about the will in my book, *A Shepherd Looks at Psalm 23*.

Suffice it to say here that my will is the key area which Christ must come to control if I am to be of any consequence in His economy. It is utterly absurd to assume or suppose that a person who is determined to do his own will can ever please God. Only as our wills are brought into harmony and submission to His will do we discover the secret of divine power and productivity.

One short, stabbing, self-sacrificing sentence sums up this whole subject: "O God, not my will, but Thine be done." There is no more potent prayer.

The person who says this, means it, and has decided he will do God's will, whatever the cost, is delighted to discover: "It is God who worketh in (me) both to will and to do of his good pleasure" (Phil. 2:13). Such a person moves and lives and has his being in Christ.

He knows and experiences genuine self-control. This is the person in whom God's love is shown in magnificent and magnanimous moderation.

What has here been discussed in some detail with respect to the soul, can be applied equally to the realm of our spirits as well as all areas of our bodily life. This the reader, if earnest about his relationship to God and others, can do for himself.

It is a matter of taking a long, hard look at the garden of my life. What is it producing? What kind of crops are coming from it? Is the Master satisfied? Is He getting what He hoped to produce? Have His efforts been in vain or is there a bountiful yield? The yield of eternal fruitage is directly proportional to the degreee in which my life is yielded to Him. The more I am available and open the more active He becomes in any given area of my life.

John the Baptist, speaking about his relationship to Christ, put it pungently when he declared boldly: "He (Christ) must increase, but I must decrease" (John 3:30). If we wish to see an increase in the fruits of God's own Spirit in our lives then it can come about only in this way. There is no other formula for fruitage. It is He and only He by His increasing presence within who can guarantee good production in generous proportion.

Lest the reader be discouraged, let it be said here again that fruit production in our Christian experience, just as in an orchard or garden, is not something that goes on with great fanfare, noise or theatrics. From the opening of the first tiny bud under the impulse of spring sunshine, to the perfect ripening of the fully formed fruit beneath late Indian summer skies in fall, the whole process goes on quietly, serenely, and surely. It is the Spirit of God who by His presence within guarantees growth, maturity, and conformity to Christ.

So gently, so gradually does this divine work of the Good Gardener proceed that often we ourselves are unaware of the changes occurring in our characters, our conversation or our conduct. But others around us are aware. They will notice the transformation taking place, and they will be aware of the ripening fruits of the Spirit in our lives. And by this they will know this garden is coming under Christ's control.

This is the ultimate, acid test of one's claim to be a Christian.

We who were once wilderness can become the garden of God!

My life is a garden.
Your life is a garden.

Is it a waste, untilled and wild?
Like an untaught, untrained child?

Or is it good soil under the Master's hand?
Is my soul His own cherished land?

Is it grown thick with thistles and weed?
Or has it been sown with His good seed?

What is the harvest that comes from this life?
Goodness and love, or hatred and strife?

O Lord, take this stony ground of mine.
Make it all, completely Thine!

Only then can it ever yield,
The pleasant fruits of a godly field.
                                        Amen and Amen.

On that day the Lord will say of his pleasant vineyard, "I watch over it and water it continually. I guard it night and day so that no one will harm it . . . "

Isaiah 27:2, 3, *Good News Bible*